DAD TIRED

AND LOVING IT

JERRAD LOPES

HARVEST HOUSE PUBLISHERS
EUGENE, OREGON

Cover design by Bryce Williamson

Cover photos © good_reason08 / Getty Images

DAD TIRED...AND LOVING IT
Copyright © 2019 by Jerrad Lopes
Published by Harvest House Publishers
Eugene, Oregon 97408
www.harvesthousepublishers.com

ISBN 978-0-7369-7716-6 (hardcover)
ISBN 978-0-7369-7717-3 (eBook)

Library of Congress Cataloging-in-Publication Data

Names: Lopes, Jerrad, author.
Title: Dad tired : and loving it / Jerrad Lopes.
Description: Eugene, Oregon : Harvest House Publishers, [2019]
Identifiers: LCCN 2019011912 (print) | LCCN 2019014448 (ebook) | ISBN 9780736977173 (ebook) | ISBN 9780736977166 (hardcover)
Subjects: LCSH: Fatherhood—Religious aspects—Christianity. Fathers—Religious life.
Classification: LCC BV4529.17 (ebook) | LCC BV4529.17 .L67 2019 (print) | DDC 248.8/421—dc23
LC record available at https://lccn.loc.gov/2019011912

Printed in the United States of America

20 21 22 23 24 25 26 27 / VP-RD / 10 9 8 7   6 5 4

To my wife, who has given me a glimpse of what God's radical grace and love look like here on earth.

To my mom, who in many ways had to be both Mom tired and Dad tired as she raised me by herself.

To my mother-in-law, who constantly watched my kids so I could find some quiet time to write this book.

And to my children, who are being used by God to help make me more like him.

CONTENTS

THE TOWEL BOY

When I was a junior in high school, I landed my first-ever job at a local gym in town. I have to admit, as a sixteen-year-old boy, it sounded pretty cool to tell your peers that you worked as a gym employee. I never really told them exactly what I did at my job; I just wanted my friends to imagine that it was something amazing. In my mind, I hoped they pictured me lifting weights and teaching other people how to get in the best shape of their lives.

The truth is, I was a towel boy.

My job was to collect the nasty, sweaty, used towels from around the facility, throw them in a giant bin, wash them, fold them, and then hand them to the members as they walked in the front door.

It was far from glamorous. In fact, most of the time it was completely disgusting, and I spent the majority of my shift trying not to vomit. But I was determined to convince my friends that I had the best job in the world—and, more importantly, that I was an expert in physical fitness.

I wasn't an expert in physical fitness, however. I was a towel boy.

I didn't possess the skills to get my friends in shape, but I could offer them a clean towel.

Sometimes when I tell people I run a ministry for young dads, I secretly hope they think I'm an expert in parenting. In my mind, I imagine they look at me as a young father who has wisdom well beyond his years.

The truth is, when it comes to parenting, I'm a towel boy.

At the time of my writing this book, I have a seven-year-old boy, a five-year-old girl, and a baby girl on the way. It would be insane for me to try to convince you that I have some secret knowledge of what it means to be a superdad.

When it comes to stumbling your way toward becoming the spiritual leader of your home, I am getting tripped up right alongside you. In fact, as I wrote this introduction, I had to pause, step away from the computer, and go yell at my kids in the front yard.

Here's the thing: As a young dad, I'm not necessarily looking for a magic formula on how to raise kids, written by someone much older than me.

> **When it comes to parenting, I'm a towel boy.**

I'll take all the advice I can get, but I also know there are no shortcuts or get-the-perfect-kid-quick methods out there.

I'm not looking for the latest parenting trends. I'm looking for Jesus.

That's why I wrote this book.

I personally wanted to know what the Scriptures had to say about what it means to lead my family well. Like many of my peers, I didn't have a dad around when I was growing up, so I had no one to teach me what spiritual leadership looks like.

This book is filled with a lot of practical tips on how to become the spiritual leader of your home, but it goes much deeper than some how-tos. It aims to get at the heart behind them.

If you have raised a child who is older than two years old, you know they all go through the "why" phase, when they question everything.

In some ways, I'm not sure I ever left the "why" stage. I know I'm supposed to be leading my family as the spiritual leader of the house, but I wanted to know why. Why did God call us to this task? And what does spiritual leadership look like today?

I don't think I'm qualified to teach you how to be the perfect dad. But I'm willing to toss you a clean towel. I'm willing to hop on the treadmill next to you and start fresh at this whole spiritual leadership thing. Most importantly, I'm willing to join you in chasing after the Perfect Father as together we learn what it means to raise children who passionately follow him.

> **I'm not looking for the latest parenting trends. I'm looking for Jesus.**

Ultimately my prayer is that by the end of this book, you will have fallen more in love with Jesus and as a result help your wife and children do the same.

I'm glad to be on this journey with you, brother. Let's start stumbling forward.

PART 1

THE KINGDOM OF GOD AROUND YOU

1

COLOR-BLIND

Why the Gospel Changes Everything

I'm color-blind.

Sometimes I find myself watching online videos of color-blind people trying on corrective color-blind glasses for the first time. In case you haven't heard, apparently someone has invented eyeglasses that can allow a color-blind person to see the world in normal color. One man's wife surprised him with a pair of these glasses as a gift, and as the viewers, we get to see his response to seeing the world in color for the first time.

At first, he's trying to play it pretty cool. As any confident man would do, he doesn't seem to act overly surprised or emotional. From behind the camera, you can hear his wife say, "Look at your kids' eyes." And that's when things take a turn. As he looks down at his daughter and stares her in the eyes, he begins to get emotional. He fights back the tears as he sees the beautiful color of his daughter's eyes for the first time.

He's a wreck. I'm a wreck. It's an emotional mess.

He was born color-blind, but now he can see. For the first time in his life, he can see how things were supposed to be.

Leila, my wife, once signed me up for a color-blind study at the local college to see if we could pull off a similar video. I spent hours in a lab failing all kinds of tests and confirming that my eyes really are broken. I tried on one pair of eyeglasses after another but with no luck. Leila stood by with her camera constantly recording my reactions. But there was nothing. They didn't have a single pair of glasses that could correct my color-blindness.

> **Sometimes I think none of us can see the world as it should be.**

To this day, I'm not able to see the world as it should be.

Sometimes I think none of us can see the world as it should be.

One of the scariest parts of our world is that nothing really surprises us anymore. Think about this: What news story would you have to hear to make you genuinely surprised or shocked? When I turn on the news or scroll through the news app on my phone, I read story after story of all kinds of evil and wickedness. But to be honest, I'm not surprised. We have heard so many terrible stories that they have become normal to us. Even something as terrible as a school shooting doesn't surprise us anymore. We almost expect it. It has become the new normal. In fact, did you know that as I'm writing this, the Columbine shooting, which is implanted deep into many of our minds, isn't even in the top ten worst shootings anymore?

The brokenness, wickedness, tragedy, and pain have become our new normal.

But it's not normal.

This isn't the way things were supposed to be.

WHERE IT ALL STARTED

My kids love the story of creation and the start of humanity told in

Genesis. We read it weekly. They are fascinated by the idea that God can make something out of nothing. They especially love the part about God walking with the humans in the garden. And of course, they giggle every time they hear that Adam and Eve were naked and unashamed.

"That's how it should be!" I constantly explain.

I am always trying to teach my kids that shame isn't normal. Hiding from God isn't normal. Feeling far from God isn't normal. Yes, those things describe *our* normal. We feel those things every day, but they aren't the way things are supposed to be.

> **The very first words we ever see from Satan are a lie.**

"Normal" in the book of Genesis, and in the story of humanity, lasts for about three chapters before things take a terrible turn for the worse.

Satan, disguised as a serpent, presents an interesting proposition to Adam and Eve: "Did God actually say, 'You shall not eat of any tree in the garden?'" (Genesis 3:1).

The very first words we ever see from Satan are a lie.

God didn't say they couldn't eat from any tree. In fact, quite the opposite: God said they could eat from any tree in the garden except one—the tree of the knowledge of good and evil.

Satan has been telling lies about God since day one. But really, he wasn't tempting Adam and Eve with a piece of fruit. Keep in mind that they are in the most glorious and robust garden in the history of the world. There is no shortage of good fruit all around them. Satan wasn't tempting them with an apple—he was tempting them with satisfaction outside of God.

Satan's goal was to convince Adam and Eve that God was holding out on them. That there was something better, more satisfying, outside of God's design. And they fell for it.

Satan tempts you and me with the same lie to this very day. He continues to plant this idea in our heads: "I wonder what life is like outside of God. I wonder if there is something better for me, something more satisfying than God alone."

His tactics are extremely effective, but they aren't new. He has had one objective from the beginning of time: to convince humans that life is best lived outside of God's design and outside of the way things are meant to be.

> **It was once normal to walk with God. Now the new normal is to run and hide from God.**

Only three chapters into the Bible, things take a radical turn for the worse. What was once normal becomes radically abnormal.

It once was normal to walk with God. Now the new normal is to run and hide from God.

It once was normal to be in relationship with God and other people without friction and shame. Now it's normal to endure friction and suffer death in relationships.

Everything that was normal, everything that was exactly how God designed it to be gets flipped on its head.

If he were anything like us, he would have bailed. He designed a perfect world, a world where we could thrive with him and each other. A world with no death, no tears, no shame, and no pain. It was perfect. And we, in our desire to pursue satisfaction outside of him, stepped out from under his design. It was our choice, not his. He could have left—and maybe he should have.

But he didn't leave.

If I were new to the Bible and heard this story for the first time, I would assume that the next few chapters would describe God going through a fit of fury. Everything that he spent time creating perfectly has just been destroyed, and the normal reaction would be for him to be really upset—maybe even destroy the humans he just created. I wouldn't be surprised to read about lightning bolts and wrath. He had every right to be furious.

But do you know what God is doing on arguably the worst day in human history?

He's taking a walk (see Genesis 3:8).

Catch this: On the worst day of the history of the world, God isn't stomping around like a toddler who just got his tablet taken away. Instead, we find him taking a walk in the garden.

Instead of running away from the mess or shouting from afar, we see the God of the universe walking with his creation on their worst day. We learn from the very first pages of Scripture that God isn't afraid to be near broken and messy people.

> **Do you know what God is doing on arguably the worst day in human history? He's taking a walk.**

Don't get me wrong—God is upset. How could he not be? He created everything and knows how it works best, and yet he is watching his creation tear things apart.

I once spent an entire week building a wooden playhouse for my kids to play in, only to find that they had taken it completely apart because they thought it would be more fun to see what the wood does if they throw it into the pool. It's frustrating when someone breaks something that you've spent so much time creating.

But somewhere hidden in the consequences, we find a glimmer of hope from our good Father. Instead of bailing, and instead of destroying

Instead of bailing,
and instead of
destroying everything,
God makes a
promise to bring
everything back to
the way things were
supposed to be.

everything, God makes a promise to bring everything back to the way things were supposed to be. In essence, God says, "Don't worry. I'm going to fix this."

A NEW NORMAL

Fast-forward thousands of years, and it's hard to find anyone in Scripture who remembers those normal days of walking in the garden with God. What once was normal now seems abnormal. And what was once abnormal seems normal.

Sickness and death weren't normal. Now everyone gets sick and eventually dies.

Murder wasn't a thing. Now you can't turn more than three pages into a story without someone killing another person.

Adultery was unheard of. Now faithfulness is a rare quality to be found.

Brokenness, evil, and wickedness have become the new normal.

There's a story in the Gospel of Mark of Jesus healing a paralyzed man. The man's friends, full of faith, are desperate to get him in front of Jesus to be healed. Unfortunately, the room is crowded with people, so they decide to cut a hole in the roof of the house and lower their friend down. That's some serious commitment. Jesus looks at the man dangling down and says, "Son, your sins are forgiven" (Mark 2:5). Jesus's words here are interesting because the man didn't come to get his sins forgiven—he came to get his legs fixed. Jesus always had a way of getting to the heart of the issue and recognizing the deeper problem at hand.

> In his kingdom, there is nothing but grace.

Jesus's talk of forgiving sins upset the religious leaders. They knew that only God could forgive sins, so for Jesus to make that statement with such authority was the greatest and boldest statement he could have made. It was a statement that would eventually lead to his death.

Listen to how the rest of the story unfolds:

> "Why does this man speak like that? He is blaspheming! Who can forgive sins but God alone?" And immediately Jesus, perceiving in his spirit that they thus questioned within themselves, said to them, "Why do you question these things in your hearts? Which is easier, to say to the paralytic, 'Your sins are forgiven,' or to say, 'Rise, take up your bed and walk'? But that you may know that the Son of Man has authority on earth to forgive sins"—he said to the paralytic—"I say to you, rise, pick up your bed, and go home." And he rose and immediately picked up his bed and went out before them all, so that they were all amazed and glorified God, saying, "We never saw anything like this!" (Mark 2:7-12).

> **Jesus wasn't being abnormal; he was showing them what normal looks like.**

"They were all amazed," Mark says. In fact, all throughout the book of Mark, you find people who are amazed by the way Jesus talked, taught, and healed.

They were amazed because it wasn't normal for them to see radical grace, unending forgiveness, or physical healing. In fact, they had never seen anything like it before. But to Jesus, this is what normal life looks like. In his kingdom, there is nothing but grace. In his kingdom, there is no such thing as sickness or death.

Jesus wasn't being abnormal; he was showing them what normal looks like. He was reminding them of how things were before humans stepped outside of his design. Jesus was giving them a pair of color-blind corrective glasses and showing them what the world was supposed to look like. He was pointing them back to normal life.

YOUR KINGDOM COME

When I was a kid, I used to think the point of being a Christian was going to heaven—or more specifically, not going to hell. I remember sitting in church one day and hearing the pastor give a lengthy sermon on how terrible hell is and how to avoid it simply by repeating a prayer after him. So like any logical person who doesn't want to be burned in a fire for all eternity, I repeated the prayer.

When I got home that night, I was nervous that I didn't truly mean the words I had said in the prayer, so I prayed it again, just to make sure God knew I was serious. I ended up praying that prayer about ten thousand more times over the next several years, constantly worried that I wasn't sincere enough or that maybe God had forgotten that I really didn't want to go to hell.

> **Jesus never asked anyone to repeat a prayer to get into heaven. He also never talked about hell to scare people into heaven.**

As I grew older, I learned that Jesus never asked anyone to repeat a prayer to get into heaven. In fact, nowhere in the Bible does anyone say that the key to salvation is to simply repeat a prayer asking Jesus into your heart. You'll also never find Jesus talking about hell to scare people into heaven.

In Matthew 6, Jesus teaches his disciples how to pray. Listen to what he says:

> Pray then like this:
> Our Father in heaven,

hallowed be your name.
Your kingdom come,
your will be done,
on earth as it is in heaven.
Give us this day our daily bread,
and forgive us our debts,
as we also have forgiven our debtors.
And lead us not into temptation,
but deliver us from evil (Matthew 6:9-13).

Check this out. In the second sentence, Jesus tells his disciples to pray that God's kingdom and his will would be done on earth as it is in heaven. Jesus didn't tell them to pray, "God, make this life go by quickly so we can experience heaven one day." No. Instead, he tells them to pray that heaven would come here to earth. Jesus is teaching his disciples that heaven isn't just a "someday" thing. It's a "here-and-now" thing too.

> **Following Jesus means we get to be part of experiencing heaven coming to earth today.**

When Jesus is preaching radical forgiveness and healing the sick, he is giving the world a glimpse of heaven. He is bringing chunks of heaven, and God's will, down here to earth. And what's crazy is that he tells his disciples to pray for the same.

Following Jesus doesn't just mean we get to avoid hell. Following Jesus means we get to be part of experiencing heaven coming to earth today.

A BIGGER STORY

You likely picked up this book to find some practical tips on how to be a better dad. But if we miss the bigger story going on around us, we will simply turn into moral adults trying to raise moral children. And that's not God's design for your life or for the lives of your children.

Amid your busy life, your stress at work, and the chaos of trying to be a husband and father, a much bigger story is unfolding around you. There is a story of God keeping the promise he made in the first pages of Scripture. He is in the process of turning things back to the way they are supposed to be. He is transforming the abnormal parts of our hearts and world, making them normal again. This is God's plan for your life. He wants nothing more than to take what has been broken in you and make it new again. And here's the crazy part: He picked you to help do the same thing in the lives of your children.

> **God doesn't want you to simply raise moral children. He wants their hearts to be radically in love with his.**

Before the creation of the world, God knew what was going to happen. He knew we would step outside his design and into a world of brokenness. He knew he would spend thousands of years on a rescue mission to recapture our hearts. And he knew he wanted to include you in the rescue of your child's heart.

God doesn't want you to simply raise moral children. He wants their hearts to be radically in love with his. In his sovereignty, and in the middle of your mess, he has chosen you to be part of that mission.

This is the good news, the gospel of Jesus Christ: God didn't bail on us but instead promised to fix the mess.

Brother, God wants to fix the mess in your heart. He wants to take your pain, your brokenness, your past, and your shortcomings and give you a new life. God is relentless in his pursuit of your heart and turning things back to the way they were designed to be. The fact that you picked up this book and are reading these words is evidence that God is still chasing after your heart. He won't stop until things are back to the way they are supposed to be.

Sometimes as tired dads, it can seem like our only objective is to survive the day. There have been many nights where I've laid my head on my pillow and tried to think about what I accomplished as a parent. It often feels like I spend most of my days saying "No!" or "Don't touch that!" or "Not right now." When I zoom in to the daily moments of my life and parenting, I am often discouraged. My guess is that as a dad, you've probably felt the same.

> There is a bigger story going on around us, a story in which God has included you.

As a follower of Jesus, I am convinced that there is more to parenting than simply surviving. If we get lost in the chaos of dirty diapers, grumpy bosses, and overflowing dishwashers, we'll lose sight of the bigger story of God's redeeming work around us. We'll forget that God is relentlessly at work fixing the brokenness of our hearts and equipping us to be part of that same work in the lives of our children.

If we miss that story, the rest of this book is pointless. On the other hand, if all you gain from this book is a bigger picture of the gospel and God's work throughout the world, it will be worth it.

You're a tired dad—I get it. I'm tired too. But let us not forget that there is a bigger story going on around us, a story in which God has included you. My prayer for my own life and for you as my brother is that these words from Paul will one day be true of us:

"I have fought the good fight, I have finished the race, I have kept the faith" (2 Timothy 4:7).

2

SATAN'S CESSPOOL

How Your Marriage
Points Your Kids to the Gospel

During the summer before my senior year of high school, some friends invited me to float down the American River to beat the excruciating heat of the California Valley. I love anything that has to do with being on the water, so I gladly agreed to join. That morning I showed up to the river in a pair of board shorts and some old flip-flops. The five of us high schoolers piled up in an inflatable raft, and my friend John joined alongside in his inflatable kayak. We spent the day slowly floating down the river, talking about all the dumb things typical high school boys talk about and making tons of inappropriate jokes.

As the sun began to set, John asked me if I wanted to try his inflatable kayak before we called it a day. That was a no-brainer. We quickly made the awkward swap of seating, trying not to fall into the water as he jumped into the raft and I climbed into his kayak. Being somewhat of a lone ranger, I decided to find out just how fast this little kayak could fly through the water, so I told my friends I'd go on ahead and meet them at the car.

Once I had made some distance between me and the group, I sat quietly in the kayak by myself, leaning back and letting the sun hit my face as the gentle current slowly moved me along. I was in my happy place.

That is, until two guys behind me broke my nirvana by yelling out, "Hey, man! Have you ever done this river before?"

"Done this river?" What the heck does that even mean? I thought to myself before turning around and seeing who was behind me. When I looked back, I saw two guys in whitewater kayaks, wearing wetsuits and helmets. *Seems like overkill,* I said to myself.

"Yeah, man, I've floated a river before," I responded with a slight bit of high-school-boy arrogance in my voice.

"Cool. Well, just be careful. Satan's Cesspool is up ahead," one of the guys said with a serious look on his face as they quickly moved past me.

Just as those words left his mouth, the current began to speed up, almost as if he controlled the flow of the river with his words. I turned my head back around to the front and squinted my eyes. In the distance, I could see some men standing on the shore with professional camera equipment, taking photos of kayaks as they dropped off the horizon.

By this time, my heart rate was racing, and so was the river's current. I watched the two guys ahead of me enter the white water and then drop into some kind of black hole. I braced myself, knowing there was no turning back at this point. I made eye contact with a professional photographer standing on shore who looked even more terrified than I did. He clearly knew I was way out of my league.

I was in an inflatable kayak with board shorts and flip-flops. No T-shirt. No life jacket. No wetsuit. And no helmet.

I've never been in a tornado before, but I imagine that if a tornado and a white-water river had a baby, it would look a lot like the chaos I entered that day.

Immediately when hitting the spiraling waterfall, my kayak folded in half and threw me out of the seat. I don't remember being in the air, but I do remember my body being scraped on the floor of the river. My head, arms, and legs hit every rock and branch as the pressure from the waterfall pushed me down to the bottom of the river floor.

For the first time in my life, I was praying *for* my life.

God, please don't let me die. Please don't let me die. Please don't let me die, I prayed repeatedly in my head. I've never felt that kind of desperation before.

The next thing I knew, I was laying on a shallow bed of rocks near the shore. Somehow, by the grace of God, the river spit me out of the current and onto the shore. I lay there in shock, trying to process what had just happened. After several minutes, I slowly stood up and started my walk back to the car, wondering how I would describe to my friends what just happened.

To this day, I regret not asking the photographer to send me those pictures. A photo of my legs sticking out of the water of a giant waterfall would make an epic Facebook profile picture.

I woke up that morning intending to enjoy a relaxing, fun-filled day on the water with my friends. I never imagined I would be fighting for my life in Satan's Cesspool.

NOT WHAT I THOUGHT IT WAS GOING TO BE

My mom and dad split up when I was three years old. I had three older sisters, the youngest of whom was five years older than me, so I was definitely the baby boy. I remember playing basketball in the driveway by myself and imagining what it would be like to have a dad watching and teaching me. Those thoughts would lead to me daydreaming about growing up and getting married one day. Even as a boy, I was excited to get married and have a family. I was eager to be the kind of dad I had always wanted and the kind of husband I wanted to see my mom with. I knew I was going to be the best husband and dad the world had ever seen.

Leila and I met when I was twenty-two. I was a young pastor who had just moved to Portland, Oregon, months earlier. Our church was hosting a Chris Tomlin concert, and Leila walked in the doors where I was greeting guests. I wanted to make sure she felt *extra* welcomed at our church that night, so I went above and beyond to accommodate her. The truth is, I thought she was stunning, and I noticed she had come in alone, so I was set on snatching her as my wife before someone else did.

> I learned that it's hard to hide in marriage—and that I had spent most of my life hiding.

I had a vision, and I'm a go-getter.

Somehow I didn't scare her away too quickly, and we ended up talking for hours.[1] Just four months later, I asked her to be my wife. I'm not kidding when I say I knew I had to marry her before someone else did. Six months after our engagement, we were married. And nine months into our marriage, we found out she was pregnant with our son, Elijah.

I was ready to start my journey as the best-ever father and husband.

But as it turns out, my good intentions could only get me so far.

My marriage ended up being a lot like my experience kayaking the American River. What I thought would be relaxing and fun-filled turned out to be more like Satan's Cesspool.

I'm kidding. That's a little intense. Obviously I would never publicly compare my marriage to Satan's Cesspool.

But I'm also not fully kidding.

---

[1] How Christian are we that we met at a Chris Tomlin concert! That could be either the coolest or the cheesiest thing ever.

Marriage wasn't what I thought it was going to be. In my mind, marriage was like hanging out with your best friend, laughing all the time, and having all kinds of adventures together. But it ended up being hard. It wasn't always fun-filled, and it most certainly wasn't always relaxing. Just like being on the kayak that day, I quickly learned that I was in over my head and way out of my league.

I learned that it's hard to hide in marriage—and that I had spent most of my life hiding. Growing up, it was easy to impress friends, coworkers, and classmates because no one fully knew me. But in marriage, I was fully known. The darkest parts of me, the most sinful things about me, were being exposed.

> **It didn't take me long to realize that God was using marriage not for my pleasure but for my holiness.**

It didn't take me long to realize that God was using marriage not for my pleasure but for my holiness. He was using my wife to expose the wickedness inside of me. And to be honest, that wasn't too relaxing. In fact, it sucked.

I remember thinking back to when I was a single guy. My sins weighed heavily on me and had consequences. But now, as a married man, my sins seemed to carry twice the weight—in fact, three times the weight once we had our son. My sinful nature didn't affect only me anymore. It deeply affected my new little family.

I'll never forget the time I had to confess to Leila that I had looked at pornography. She was devastated. Her heart was crushed. It was the first time I realized that marriage wasn't going to be a relaxing float down a river. Instead, it would be full of white water that would sometimes flip me out of my boat.

I wish I could say that was the only time I've broken my wife's heart, but

I'd be lying. We're only a decade into marriage, and I've lost count of how many times I've hurt her, broken her trust, and said harsh words that have crushed her spirit.

I'm not the best husband and dad. I have fallen incredibly short of the man I imagined I would be. And the truth is, especially by the world's standards, Leila has had every right to leave me.

But she didn't leave. And she won't leave. She's been faithful.

PUSHING THROUGH THE RAPIDS

We seem to be attending a lot of weddings these days. Many of our friends are getting married and starting families. Because I'm a pastor, I am often asked to officiate weddings for our friends. (I think they often ask because they know they don't have to pay me. I'll gladly accept the free dinner instead.)

> **God had every right to leave humanity, but he didn't. He stuck around.**

Some guys don't like weddings, but I really enjoy them. I'm kind of sappy and get caught up in all the young love. It reminds me of what it was like when I first met Leila and all the excitement we had starting our lives together.

But amid the excitement, sometimes I feel as if the bride and groom come to the wedding in board shorts and a pair of old flip-flops. Not literally, of course (although that would probably be the most fun wedding I'd ever attend).

What I mean is that sometimes I feel like the bride and groom show up naive. I feel like they are walking into marriage with the idea that they'll be enjoying a relaxing float down the river together. I just want to toss them wetsuits and helmets and yell, "You're about to fall into Satan's Cesspool!"

You don't have to be
married long
to realize that marriage
isn't the thing that will
bring you the most joy.
It won't satisfy
the deepest longings
of your soul.

Because the truth is, marriage is hard. Many of us walked into married life with blinders on. We expected it to be one thing and learned that it's quite another. You don't have to be married long to realize that marriage isn't the thing that will bring you the most joy. It won't satisfy the deepest longings of your soul.

> **If God treated us the way we traditionally have treated the marriage relationship, the Bible would only be one page long.**

I think this is where most divorces begin. When people realize that their spouses aren't as great as they initially thought they were or that marriage isn't as great as they hoped it would be, they start to look for joy elsewhere.

"There are plenty of fish in the sea. Maybe I picked the wrong one," a guy once told me. I've heard of people encouraging a member of their extended family to get a divorce because the spouse hurt their relative or no longer makes the person happy.

If the standard for marriage is joy, then Leila should have left me a long time ago. We have spent seasons of our relationship together without joy. Yet she didn't leave. And in her faithfulness, she gave me and our children a glimpse of the gospel.

Just as she had every right to leave, but she didn't, God had every right to leave humanity, but he didn't. He stuck around.

If God treated us the way we traditionally have treated the marriage relationship, the Bible would only be one page long:

> God makes a perfect world.
> Humans turn their back on him.
> God gets angry and leaves.
> The end.

But our Bible is thousands of pages long because we serve a God who was willing to kick down a lot of doors to get things back to the way they were supposed to be. In fact, throughout Scripture, we see God refer to himself as our groom and us as his bride. He is a groom on a mission to rescue a bride who has turned her back on him.

"For your Maker is your husband, the LORD of hosts is his name" (Isaiah 54:5).

"And in that day, declares the LORD, you will call me 'My Husband'" (Hosea 2:16).

"I saw the holy city, new Jerusalem, coming down out of heaven from God, prepared as a bride adorned for her husband" (Revelation 21:2).

> **You and I are the bride of Christ, and we are a terrible bride. We have turned our backs on the groom and looked for love in other places.**

The Bible is not a random story of a majestic being interacting with humans from afar. The Scriptures reveal a love story in which the God of the universe compares himself to a groom chasing after his undeserving wife with relentless love.

This is what Paul means in Ephesians 5 when he tells us to love our brides the way Christ loves the church. He's not encouraging a sappy, superficial love based on our feelings and emotions. He's talking about a relentless love that will do whatever it takes to pursue his bride.

Here's the thing: You and I are the bride of Christ, and we are a terrible bride. We have turned our backs on the groom and looked for love in other places. We most certainly have not been faithful to him despite his faithfulness to us. And just like Adam and Eve back in the garden, we have stepped out from under his design and sought satisfaction from creation rather than the Creator.

God should have given up on us. But he didn't.

And here's the good news, bro. You are fully known and also fully loved. God not only chose you but also knows everything about you—and still sticks around. He knows your sins, your wicked thoughts, and your deceitful heart. He knows you intimately and loves you passionately.

That's seriously amazing.

> **God not only chose you but also knows everything about you—and still sticks around. He knows you intimately and loves you passionately.**

Think about that for a second.

God doesn't just tolerate you or put up with you—he loves you. In the middle of your mess, he loves you fully.

That's *really* good news.

Years ago, a friend called me late at night and asked if he could come to my house to talk. He was in the middle of a rough season of marriage and needed someone to process with. He sat on my couch for more than an hour and talked about how hard it was for him to love his wife.

"She is so selfish. She disrespects me, always makes demands of me, and never wants to give anything in return. She has such a high standard for me but hardly any standard for herself as a wife. Plus, I couldn't even tell you the last time we had sex."

He was exhausted, angry, and overwhelmed.

"That sucks, man. I'm really sorry," I said. "But I feel like I have to remind you of the gospel. You are the bride of Christ, and I'm assuming you've been pretty selfish toward God, demanding much of him but wanting to do little in return. You've expected him to show up for you in major ways, but you didn't hold up your end of the deal. And the truth is, he should have bailed on you. He had every right to leave you in your mess. He had every right to give up on you. But he didn't. God, even in this very moment, loves you passionately and continues to pursue your heart. That's how he wants you to love your wife. You've got to go home and continue to lay down your life because Jesus laid down his life for you."

I gospel-slapped him.

And he hated it just as much as I would hate it if someone gave me that advice. Because everything in us just wants to be served. We want people to lay down their lives for us, not the other way around.

> **God doesn't just tolerate you or put up with you—he loves you. In the middle of your mess, he loves you fully.**

Dying sucks. And yet we're called to do it every single day.

That was hard for him to hear that night, and I imagine it's hard for you to read. You may be going through a really hard time in your marriage, and you can't imagine "dying" another day. You've been dying for months, maybe years, and you don't think you have anything more to give.

Let me give you some good news.

I once had a mentor who told me that the greatest gift you can give your children is to love their mother well. To be honest, that didn't really make sense to me as a young husband and dad. But here's what I've learned: The greatest gift you can give your children is Jesus. And the best way to point them toward Jesus is by loving your wife like Jesus loves the church.

As the spiritual leader of your home, there is no better way to give your kids a practical glimpse of the gospel than to love your wife with the same relentless love God has given you. When my kids watch my wife, who knows me fully, love me with everything she has, they get to see a picture of God's love for us. When they see me passionately pursue their mom every day, despite her imperfections, they are getting a glimpse of what it looks like for God to pursue them every day despite their imperfections.

When my kids see that Mommy and Daddy know each other fully and love each other fully, they are getting a glimpse of the gospel.

This was God's design for marriage. It was never about happiness. It was about holiness. Your marriage was designed by God to help you become more like him and also to give you—and the world—a picture of his amazing love for us.

> **As the spiritual leader of your home, there is no better way to give your kids a practical glimpse of the gospel than to love your wife with the same relentless love God has given you.**

If I left my wife when things were hard or if she left me when she was unhappy, we wouldn't be giving our kids an accurate view of the gospel. God stayed when things were hard, so we stay when things are hard. God pursues us with passion, so we pursue each other with passion.

Your marriage is way bigger than your joy. It's way bigger than you. If you can learn to love your wife with the kind of love Jesus has for you, you will do what no Bible study, Sunday school class, or nightly devotional can do: You will have given your children a real-life picture of what God's love is like toward them.

That's why loving your wife is the greatest gift you can give your kids. It will point them to the greatest love of all time. It will point them toward Jesus. And that gift will last forever.

Marriage really is like Satan's Cesspool. It's chaotic, and messy, and even scary at times. Satan would like nothing more than to destroy you. But Satan doesn't have to win, because as followers of Jesus, as citizens of his kingdom, we get to give our children a glimpse of the gospel. We can zip up our wetsuits and strap on our helmets and let life toss us around. But we won't drown. We won't quit. We won't give up. We'll push through the rapids because Jesus pushed down every obstacle he needed to in order to get to us. We won't stop pursuing our wives, because Christ didn't stop pursuing us. And we won't give up, even when things seem impossible, because Christ didn't give up on us.

LISTS WON'T WORK

I know you may read this and get inspired to go love your wife but then have no idea what to do. Maybe you didn't grow up with a dad around or a man to show you what it looks like to pursue your wife the way Jesus pursues the church. So I want to give you some really practical ways you can do this. But before I do, I think it's important to remember that Scripture simply says to love your wife the way Christ loves the church. God didn't give us a magical checklist to follow as a husband. Instead of telling us exactly what to do, he gave us the heartbeat behind why we do it.

> That's why loving your wife is the greatest gift you can give your kids.

Imagine I want to be a better husband to Leila, so I buy a book called *101 Ways to Be a Better Husband*. I crack it open, and on day one, it tells me to go buy her flowers. So I head to Costco[2] and pick up a couple dozen roses, put them in a vase, and place them on the table for her to see when she walks in the door.

"Oh my gosh! They're beautiful!" she says when she comes home.

---

[2] Seriously, this is the best place to buy flowers. They're super affordable and always of good quality. You're welcome.

When my kids
see that
Mommy and Daddy
know each other fully
and love each other fully,
they are getting
a glimpse
of the gospel.

"I'm glad you like them. I just bought a book that tells me how to be a better husband, and this was my first task," I reply.

Immediately the quality of my gift decreases.

The next day, I open the book to chapter 2 and read that I should clean the house because wives typically like a clean home. I spend the rest of the day cleaning the house, making sure every square foot is perfectly organized.

Leila walks in the door and nearly gets tears in her eyes.

"Wow, babe! This is amazing! Did you seriously sacrifice all day to clean the house for me?" she says.

"Yep! Chapter 2 of the book I'm reading says you'd like a clean house, so I did what it says," I respond.

Again, my gift loses its value. In fact, it almost becomes offensive. My wife appreciates the gift, but she wants more. She wants my heart.

> **He doesn't want you to follow a list to be in love with him—he wants your heart.**

This is why the Scriptures don't give us a list to follow. Instead, the apostle Paul simply tells us to love our wives the way Christ loved the church. Did Jesus follow a list when loving you? No, he gave it everything he had. He doesn't want you to follow a list to be in love with him—he wants your heart. And your wife doesn't want you to follow a list of rules either. She wants your heart.

As you read the next few sections, keep in mind that every marriage is different. What feels loving to one person may not feel the same to another. Your wife is uniquely designed by God. Study her. Become a student of how God has wired her. Find out the unique ways she feels loved and go all-in on those.

SHORT-TERM MEMORY

In one of my favorite passages of Scripture (Exodus 6), the Israelites are wandering in the desert and beginning to grumble. God has just miraculously rescued them from slavery in Egypt and is leading them to a better land, but they are hungry and unhappy. They figure maybe it would have been better to remain as slaves and have food than to be with God and die from starvation. So God, being gracious, rains down bread from heaven so they have enough food to eat. He tells them to just take enough bread for the day because he will be providing food for them each day. God is testing them to see whether they will be obedient to his command or hoard more food than they need for that day.

> **The God we serve doesn't stop pursuing our hearts, even once we have been saved.**

This passage has always been interesting to me because God could have easily given them enough food for several days—or weeks. But he chooses to only give them enough for one day at a time. God wanted the Israelites to have a daily dependence and a daily interaction with him. The God of the entire world, who is making sure the stars stay aligned and the oceans stay in rhythm, somehow still has the desire to interact with his people every single day.

This is incredible.

Throughout the Bible, we see God interacting with humanity on a consistent basis. He doesn't just ask us to say a prayer and then leave us on our own. Instead, he invites us into a lifelong relationship with him.

"Even to your old age I am he, and to gray hairs I will carry you" (Isaiah 46:4).

Every year, every day, every hour, the God we serve doesn't stop pursuing our hearts, even once we have been saved.

This is the model God gave you for loving your wife. You don't get to just put a ring on her finger and then coast from there. Loving your wife the way God has loved you means chasing after her heart every single day. It means pursuing her until your hairs turn gray (which started sooner than most of us thought it would). It means loving her enough to wake up every morning and chase after her heart the way God chases after yours every single day.

Last year I took Leila on a cruise for our wedding anniversary. It was the most amazing trip. We spent seven days together, kid-free, on a romantic boat sailing the ocean. We laughed our heads off, dreamed about the future, and ate way more food than we should have.

I came home from that trip feeling incredibly connected to my wife. I was sure that such a big and amazing vacation would carry us for at least three or four months.

> **Loving your wife the way God has loved you means chasing after her heart every single day.**

Turns out it lasted about two days. Then we were back into the normal swing of life and back to the daily challenges of parenting and marriage. That big vacation couldn't sustain us. We needed more than a big vacation—we needed a daily pursuit of each other's hearts.

You need to date your wife, and you need to date her often. But even more than that, you need to figure out how to connect with her every day. What would it look like in your marriage to have a small connection with your wife each day?

Maybe it means greeting your wife first, before the kids, when you come home from work—giving her a kiss, holding her in your arms, and having a short connection each day.

Maybe it means turning your bedroom into a no-phone space. After you put the kids to bed, charge your cell phone in a different room. Spend thirty to sixty minutes of quality time each night with your wife. Pray for her, ask her about her day, and connect intimately.

Whatever you decide, make it intentional and build it into a normal part of your daily routine. It doesn't have to be a grand gesture, but it does need to be intentional, and it needs to happen daily.

THE REAL PROTECTOR

Most guys take a lot of pride in their role as protector and provider. I've yet to meet a man who would hesitate to lay down his life for his family if the situation arose.

But here's the thing: Statistically, you will most likely never be in a situation that requires you to give up your life for your family, and I pray that this is never a reality for you. And as cool as it may sound to say that you'd die for the ones you love, the chances of this happening are slim to none.

> **The scary part is that Satan hasn't stopped whispering lies into your wife's ears.**

Remember Genesis 3, the garden scene with Adam and Eve? The serpent slithers up to Eve and begins to whisper lies about her identity. He convinces her that God is holding out on her and that if she eats of the fruit, she'll find more satisfaction than she's currently finding in God alone. She buys into the lie and eats of the fruit. "She also gave some to her husband who was with her, and he ate" (Genesis 3:6).

Imagine the scene. Satan is tempting Eve, and Adam is standing there in silence. He doesn't say a word.

The scary part is that Satan hasn't stopped whispering lies into your wife's ears. To this very day, he is trying to convince your wife that she can find more satisfaction than she is finding in Christ alone.

If she weighed less.

If she were prettier.

If she were smarter.

If she were a better mom.

If she were a better wife.

If she had more friends.

If she had a better house.

Every day, the same serpent that whispered lies into Eve's ears is whispering these lies into your wife's ears. And either we will be passive husbands like Adam, who stand around and watch, or we will be men of God who step in and protect.

This is what protection looks like for a godly husband who wants to lead his family well.

"For we do not wrestle against flesh and blood, but against the rulers, against the authorities, against the cosmic powers over this present darkness, against the spiritual forces of evil in the heavenly places" (Ephesians 6:12).

Your enemy wants more than to cause physical harm to your family. Your enemy continues to lie to your wife day and night, convincing her that Jesus isn't enough.

> **Every day,
> the same serpent
> that whispered lies
> into Eve's ears
> is whispering
> these lies into
> your wife's ears.**

If you are serious about protecting your wife, commit to praying with and for her. Set aside time each week to pray against the lies of the enemy. Pray that God will remind her that she is loved and delighted in, not because she's pretty or an awesome mom, but because she is a daughter of the Most High King.

As husbands, we fight for our wives by bringing them before the ultimate protector, Christ. We ask that the Holy Spirit will do what we can't do—remind her constantly of who she is in Christ and that she is loved, cherished, delighted in, and valuable because of what Jesus did on the cross.

If you want to get practical, set a daily reminder on your phone to remind you to pray for her each day. Unless you're crazy intentional, this will likely remain just a good idea but not part of your family routine.

BOTTOM LINE

> If we are amazing fathers but don't love our wives well, we will fail to give our kids everything they need.

Here's the hard reality: If we are amazing fathers but don't love our wives well, we will fail to give our kids everything they need. They need a great father, but that's only showing them one part of the gospel. They also need a father who will take seriously the role of loving his wife the way Christ loves the church. They need a daddy who relentlessly pursues their mom the way Jesus relentlessly pursues us. The most powerful picture you will give your children of being fully known and fully loved is to let them watch Mommy and Daddy fully know and fully love each other.

This is what it means to show your kids the gospel. This is what it looks like to have the kingdom of heaven come to earth. This is the way things are supposed to be.

3

FOOTBALL JERSEYS

What's the Goal of Parenting?

When I was a kid, I grew up playing soccer. I secretly wanted to be a star football player, but my mom wouldn't let me play. She was worried I'd get hit too hard and end up with a brain injury. Honestly, I wasn't excited about guys twice my size chasing after me and trying to hit me as hard as they could. I'm not really built like a football player. My good friend Cedric played in the NFL, and sometimes I feel myself hurting when he simply looks at me wrong.

In high school, our soccer team practiced directly across the field from the football team. Every day I would look over at those guys and think about how much cooler they looked than we did. During my freshman year, I remember an older football player walking down the hall in his jersey and how all the girls stared at him like he was a movie star.

As a freshman boy, I wanted the girls to look at me like that too. But soccer players didn't really get that kind of attention at my school.

One day at practice, I decided to take matters into my own hands. I knew that even though I didn't have any football experience, I was pretty good at kicking a ball.

Surely they need a kicker, I thought to myself.

And I really needed a football jersey so I could walk down the halls wearing it.

Without really thinking, I ditched my soccer practice and ran toward the football field. I went straight up to the coach and asked him if I could try out to be the kicker of his football team. To my surprise, he simply said, "Sure, we need a kicker," and let me on the team.

I finally had a football jersey, and you better believe I wore that thing around campus like a medal of honor.

I spent the rest of the season showing up to the games and kicking the extra points after each touchdown. It was a pretty easy gig, and I appreciated getting to wear my jersey in the halls before each game on Fridays. Our team was especially good that year, so there wasn't much pressure on my end to perform well. My job was to show up, wear my jersey, and kick a ball from time to time.

That is, until October 19, 2001, when everything went downhill quickly.

It was the fourth quarter, and we were destroying the other team 56-0. I was sitting on the sidelines, minding my own business, when the coach turned around and yelled, "Lopes, you're in!"

We hadn't scored a touchdown on that series, so I knew it wasn't my turn to go in and kick the extra point. I had no clue what he was talking about, so I sat there and stared at him with confusion written all over my face.

"Lopes, put your helmet on! You're in the game!" he repeated.

I quickly realized that because we were ahead by so many points and the season was coming to a close, the coach was taking out the starters and letting the other players get as much playing time as possible.

The thing is, I didn't want more playing time. I just wanted a jersey.

I hesitantly ran onto the field without a clue of what was going on. The team huddled up, and the quarterback began to yell out some random sequence of words and letters that made no sense to me. Before I could comprehend what was happening, all the players clapped their hands at the same time and ran off to their assigned positions.

I stood next to the quarterback with a blank stare on my face.

"I have no clue what's going on," I said to him.

"Ball's coming to you, Lopes," he replied.

"I'm sorry…what?" I said in a panic.

"The ball is coming to you—get ready to catch it!" he yelled back.

I slowly walked away, terrified by what was about to happen. I was literally shaking as I lined up to start the play.

"Hike!" the quarterback yelled, and he turned to look at me.

We made eye contact, and I immediately began to shake my head, trying to indicate to him that I had no desire to catch the ball.

Apparently he didn't understand what I was trying to say, because he threw the ball as hard as he could in my direction.

I caught the ball and turned around, only to find two defensive players twice my size staring right back at me. I'm pretty sure they were foaming at the mouth.

Now, I'm not the sharpest crayon in the box, but I'm smart enough to know that any normal person doesn't run *into* danger. They run *away* from it. So being the wise ninety-five-pound, fifteen-year-old boy that I was, I quickly started to run away from the defensive players.

In the wrong direction.

The closer they got to me, the farther I ran away.

Eventually I was tackled by my own teammates before making it to the wrong end zone.

I lost sixty-five yards on the play. Needless to say, that was the last time I touched a football.

ARE YOU BLESSED?

One of my biggest "dad fears" is that I'm wearing the "Jesus jersey" but running toward the wrong end zone with my kids.

I think it's easy to say we love Jesus and want our children to also love Jesus. But honestly, it doesn't always seem like our goals as Christians look any different from the goals of those around us.

I listened to a podcast this week about over-parenting our kids. The speaker, a well-known child psychologist, shared a story about how she had recently given a speech titled "The Average Child" at a popular parenting conference. As a bestselling author, her presentations are always well attended, but for this session, not a single person showed up.

> One of my biggest "dad fears" is that I'm wearing the "Jesus jersey" but running toward the wrong end zone with my kids.

Not one person.

Who wants an average child? No one. We want exceptional children. We don't just want them to have a team jersey; we want them to be the best, the smartest, the funniest, the prettiest, and the most athletic. For many of us, the deepest desires for our children are for them to be happy, healthy, and successful.

The problem is, this isn't how the Bible defines success for us as Christ followers.

The book of Matthew tells the story of Jesus giving his first sermon. The crowd and his disciples have gathered around him in anticipation. For years, they have waited for a savior to come, and there are rumors that Jesus might actually be the guy they've been waiting for. I can't imagine what that moment would have been like for them. I picture the crowd being on the edge of their seats. Maybe you could have heard a pin drop as Jesus took a breath and began to share the first words of his ministry.

> Blessed are the poor in spirit, for theirs is the kingdom
>   of heaven.
> Blessed are those who mourn, for they shall be comforted.
> Blessed are the meek, for they shall inherit the earth.
> Blessed are those who hunger and thirst for righteousness, for they
>   shall be satisfied.
> Blessed are the merciful, for they shall receive mercy.
> Blessed are the pure in heart, for they shall see God.
> Blessed are the peacemakers, for they shall be called sons of God.
> Blessed are those who are persecuted for righteousness' sake,
>   for theirs is the kingdom of heaven.
> Blessed are you when others revile you and persecute you and
>   utter all kinds of evil against you falsely on my account.
>   Rejoice and be glad, for your reward is great in heaven,
>   for so they persecuted the prophets who were before you
>   (Matthew 5:3-12).

Are you serious? *These* are the first words of Jesus's ministry?

They had waited for hundreds of years for their king to show up—a powerful king; a king who would set up a powerful kingdom and rule the world; a king who would save them, rescue them from oppression, and lead them into victory.

Yet Jesus's first words are "Blessed are the poor in spirit..."

He goes on to say that the blessed are the meek, the hungry, those who are mourning, and those who are persecuted.

This would have made no sense to his audience. In their culture, this was the opposite of blessing. To them, you were blessed if you had lots of money, power, and status.

As it turns out, not much has changed in two thousand years.

Get on Instagram and search for #blessed. I have a feeling you're not going to find many pictures of people who are mourning and being persecuted.[1] Instead, you'll most likely find photos of people taking selfies with their new cars or houses. Or people enjoying margaritas and ocean views while on vacation. Or maybe someone who just got good news at the doctor's office.

> **Jesus's definition of blessing should rattle us the same way it probably rattled his listeners that day.**

For us, a blessing is anything that gets us closer to our goals. And many of our goals are probably the same as the goals of Jesus's audience: health, wealth, and happiness. When we get a new house, it takes us one step higher on the social ladder. When we get a good report at the doctor's office, it gets us closer to our goal of enjoying long and healthy lives. When our kids get trophies, it gets us closer to our goal of being exceptional parents with exceptional children.

We're #blessed.

But Jesus's definition of blessing should rattle us the same way it probably rattled his listeners that day.

Why in the world would Jesus say we are blessed if we are poor, sad, meek, hungry, and persecuted?

The reality of his words hit me square in the face while I was on a trip to Kenya several years ago. We had spent a week there building a fence around a man-made water source because just that year, twenty-two children had

---

[1] If you do, tag me (@dad.tired).

been killed by crocodiles while trying to fetch water for their families to drink. Our team of contractors and engineers was trying to figure out a way to redirect the water source to a fenced-in area so the people of the village could get water without the risk of being eaten.

If you feel like your problems are big right now, let that reality sink in for a minute.

During our trip, we worked alongside the locals who were also followers of Jesus. I was constantly amazed by their faith and trust in God. They prayed harder, worshipped more, and had more joy than anyone I had ever seen.

At the end of the trip, our team gathered to share stories of what we had seen and learned. I'll never forget hearing one man say to the group, "This week I learned how blessed we really are with what God has given us. I realized that we have so much at home, and we take it for granted."

> **In the kingdom of Jesus, our goal is no longer money, wealth, power, or happiness. Our goal is to know him.**

I appreciated his honest reflection, but something in me wanted to scream, "We aren't the blessed ones—they are!"

Yes, we have more stuff. And more money in our bank accounts. And even the amazing gift of clean water. But they knew the God of the Bible in a way that I didn't.

This is what I think Jesus meant when he said, "Blessed are those who mourn" and those who are poor, meek, hungry, and persecuted. Jesus was naming his disciples' goals (and ours) and flipping them on their head. In the kingdom of Jesus, our goal is no longer money, wealth, power, or happiness. Our goal is to know him.

As Christians, our *only* goal is Jesus.

The people I met in Kenya were blessed because they were meek, and that forced them to rely on God in ways I had never imagined. They were blessed because their brokenness forced them to look outside themselves for what they needed and to look to God as their true source of hope and provision.

You may be wondering, *So is it a sin to have wealth, health, or happiness?* And my answer would be no.

Most of the time.

I have met people who have a lot of money, good health, and a contagious joy, and all of that seems to point them toward Jesus. Their wealth, health, and happiness help them get closer to their goal of falling more in love with Jesus. These people seem to have a way of leveraging their money and energy to advance God's kingdom. They see themselves and everything they own as tools to bring pieces of heaven down here to earth.

But let's be honest. Those people are very few and far between. They are the exception, not the majority.

Think about your own life for a minute. Most of us will drink clean water today. We will eat good meals, drive cars, and sleep in warm beds with roofs over us. And because of this, we find ourselves praying very little. We have subconsciously convinced ourselves that we don't really need God. We have started to believe that our needs are met through our hard work and big bank accounts, not through the God who feeds the birds and numbers the hairs on our heads.

I'm willing to bet that your most faithful seasons of prayer have come in the hardest seasons of your life. If you're like me, you find yourself praying most when you are totally out of control and you need God to show up. Our money, wealth, and happiness don't usually draw us closer to God. They typically take us away from him because we start to convince ourselves that we don't really need him. It's extremely subtle and something we hate to admit, but we start to live as if we are better at being god than God is.

This is why you are blessed when you are mourning, broken, and totally out of control—because you find yourself coming back to God in ways that you didn't when everything was going smoothly. You are blessed because you are getting closer to your goal. You are getting closer to Jesus.

I think this is what the apostle Paul is getting at when he says, "Brothers, I do not consider that I have made it my own. But one thing I do: forgetting what lies behind and straining forward to what lies ahead, I press on toward the goal for the prize of the upward call of God in Christ Jesus" (Philippians 3:13-14).

> **Our children don't need health, wealth, and happiness—they need Jesus.**

Or when he says, "To me to live is Christ, and to die is gain" (Philippians 1:21).

Paul is pressing on toward his goal of getting closer to Jesus. He even goes so far as to say that if he is alive, he will live for Christ, but if he dies, he is gaining something better. This is crazy! Death is a "gain" only if Jesus is your goal. Paul was arrested, beaten, and eventually beheaded for his faith in Christ. But whether living or dying, he was getting closer to his goal: Jesus.

When I read passages like this, I start to think that Paul's goals look a lot different from ours. Most of my peers and I like the idea of our kids loving God, but we *really* love the idea of them being the smartest kids in their classes, the most talented kids on their teams, or the cutest kids in the photos.

Bro, we're running toward the wrong end zone. If we're not tackled quickly, I'm afraid we'll find ourselves at the ends of our lives having raised children who are morally pure but spiritually drained. We will have raised kids who know how to behave well yet still long for something more to satisfy their souls. Our children don't need health, wealth, and happiness—they need Jesus. As Christians, our goal isn't to raise the smartest, most successful, or most moral children. Our goal is to raise disciples of Jesus who are madly in love with him.

> **Salvation in Jesus lasts forever. It's the only goal our hearts should long for.**

In her book *Praying the Scriptures for Your Children*, Jodie Berndt says, "Praying for your children's salvation is asking God to give them the only gift that lasts forever."[2]

A successful career won't last forever. A large retirement fund won't last forever. A first-place trophy won't last forever.

Salvation in Jesus lasts forever. It's the only goal our hearts should long for.

THEY'RE ALWAYS WATCHING

So what does it actually mean to raise disciples of Jesus who are in love with him?

The word "disciple" isn't one you hear often outside of the Christian community. When we think of disciples, we typically think of the twelve dudes who followed Jesus around. But at its core, the word simply refers to someone who follows a teacher. In many ways, we are all disciples of someone or something. We have been led and influenced by all sorts of people. And whether we like it or not, most of us could be considered disciples of our friends, our bosses, our old classmates, and even our spouses. From the time we were children, we have been watching and learning from others to find our way in this world. That's what kids do: They watch and they learn. This is fundamentally what it means to be a disciple: to watch, to learn, and to imitate what we've been taught.

John, a member of our Dad Tired online community, recently shared a

---

[2] Jodie Berndt, *Praying the Scriptures for Your Children* (Grand Rapids, MI: Zondervan, 2001), chapter 1, "Praying for Your Child's Salvation."

story with me about how he caught his daughter imitating him. He admitted he had an anger problem, and when he would lose his patience with his daughter, he would hold her head in his hands and press his forehead against hers, making sure he had her full attention. He could see the fear in her eyes as she was getting in trouble. One day, he had noticed that his daughter was doing the same thing to the other kids in the neighborhood when she was frustrated with them. His heart broke because he knew she was only doing what she had seen her daddy do to her.

When it comes to training our children, more is caught than taught. Beyond any long lectures we make them listen to or any attempt to capitalize on every teachable moment with some encouraging words, they will learn most by simply watching us. They are learning more from what we do than what we say.

The scary reality is that you don't have to start discipling your kids—they are already learning from your every move. The question then becomes, What kind of disciple are you making?

I'm sure you can think of plenty of examples in your own life when, like John, you've caught your children acting like you in some way. Sometimes it's cute, like when they laugh the way you do or imitate the way you walk. My heart still melts every time I watch my daughter sit on the bathroom counter and pretend to put on her own makeup as she watches my wife get ready next to her.

> The scary reality is, you don't have to start discipling your kids—they are already learning from your every move.

There are many times, however, when you see your children mimicking your behavior for the worse, and it isn't so cute. Maybe it's a cuss word they heard you say, a look you've given, or a sin you've committed.

Few things are more heartbreaking than to see your child sin as a result of copying the things they've learned from you. We've all been there. And whether we like it or not, we are making little disciples who end up looking a lot like us. They are constantly watching and learning how to respond to life by the way we behave.

There's no getting around it—your children are constantly watching.

I challenge you to take a moment right now to courageously and honestly ask yourself what your kids see as they're watching you. What would they say you're most passionate about? What would they say matters most to their daddy? What would they say are your goals for yourself, for their mom, and for your family?

> We've all been there. And whether we like it or not, we are making little disciples who end up looking a lot like us.

I've always said that when I die, I don't want my kids to talk about how awesome I was. Instead, I want them to talk about how awesome God is. In my heart, my goal is to simply be used by God in the lives of my children to point them toward him.

Honestly though, at this point in my parenting, I'm not sure this is the message they're getting from me. It sounds great in my heart, but it doesn't seem to play out the way I want it to.

If I mustered up the courage to ask my kids what they think is most important to me, they'd probably say…

"Your work."

"Your phone."

"The *Dad Tired* podcast."

"A clean house."

"Not being too loud."

"Being obedient."

And maybe "Mexican food."

I tell them that my goal is Jesus, but by the way I live my life, they probably see me running in the wrong direction.

The question isn't whether we are leading our children. Rather, it's what we are leading them toward. If we're not intentional about leading our families toward Jesus, we will unintentionally drift in the wrong direction.

Brother, our kids need us to lead them toward Jesus. They need us to help them become Jesus's disciples.

PASSION IS CONTAGIOUS

A few months ago, I was browsing through Netflix and came across a show called *Friday Night Tikes*. It's a reality show that highlights young football teams in Texas that are trying to win a championship. At first, I chuckled as I watched how serious the parents and coaches were, treating the kids as if they were NFL players trying to win the Super Bowl. It seemed so ridiculous to me that these adults would devote five or six days a week to teaching eight-year-olds how to play a game. Their entire lives revolved around football, and they spent an absurd amount of time pursuing that goal.

> If we're not intentional about leading our families toward Jesus, we will unintentionally drift in the wrong direction.

But then something crazy happened.

The thirty-minute episode led to a binge that lasted most of the night. I watched the entire season. I cheered out loud for these kids, and to my extreme embarrassment, I even shed a tear of joy as my favorite team of eight-year-old boys won the championship.

The next morning, as I ate a bowl of cereal at the kitchen table, I asked myself, *Why the heck did I get into that show so much?* Maybe it was because it was so well produced. Or that through these kids, I was living out my childhood dreams to be a star football player. And then I was immediately struck by this thought: We lead our kids toward the things that matter most to us.

Those parents and coaches loved football more than anything else in the world. And as a result, they wanted their kids to love football more than anything else in the world. They wanted their *kids* to have what *they* desired. And the crazy part is that their passion was so strong and contagious that even I found myself wanting what they desired.

> **We lead our kids toward the things that matter most to us.**

Passion is powerful. It's contagious. It can bring others alongside it and motivate them toward a common goal.

If we're passionate about filling up our bank accounts, we seem to get passionate about our kids being successful in school so they too can make a lot of money when they're older. If we're passionate about the way we look, we seem to get passionate about our kids being the cutest and trendiest kids among their peers. If we're passionate about sports, we tend to sign our kids up for every athletic program and invest a crazy amount of time and energy into it. If we're passionate about happiness and comfort, we tend to protect our kids from hardship and give them anything that will make them happy, even if we know it's just for a short time.

Our kids often end up loving the things we love and, maybe even worse, not loving the things we don't love.

That morning at the breakfast table, I came to the realization that if my kids aren't as passionate about Jesus as I'd like them to be, maybe it's because I'm not as passionate about Jesus as I say I am.

I was immediately humbled to my core.

THE SNICKERS BAR

Several years ago, I was in Serbia training a group of pastors. After several long days of teaching sessions, I asked if we could take a break to have them show me around the city.

The pastors and their wives agreed to spend the next few hours walking me around their city, and they showed it off with great pride. After walking around awhile, we stopped by a local grocery store to pick up a snack and some drinks. As we were checking out, I told the group I'd like to buy each of them a treat as a thank-you for their generous hospitality.

As we were walking back to the church, one of the pastors' wives offered to share a piece of her Snickers bar with me...a candy bar I had just paid for at the grocery store.

Our kids often end up loving the things we love and, maybe even worse, not loving the things we don't love.

"Please, enjoy this with me," she said.

"Oh no, that's okay! Enjoy it—I got it for you," I replied.

"No, no. Please, take some of this," she insisted.

"Really, that's okay. It's yours, and I want you to enjoy it."

This back-and-forth dialogue lasted for about three minutes before she stopped walking and looked me straight in the eyes. I could see she was starting to tear up.

"Jerrad, in our country, we never enjoy good things alone. I insist that you enjoy this with me."

I realized at that moment that this wasn't about a candy bar. Something much deeper was happening. She simply couldn't imagine keeping something good to herself. She knew that the best things in life were meant to be shared.

I often think back to that story as I try to raise my children to become passionate followers of Jesus.

Sometimes I think I casually offer them a piece of Jesus to take or leave. We do church on Sundays. We pray around the dinner table. And we talk about his Word from time to time. It's almost as if I am subconsciously saying, "You want some of this? No? Okay, no problem. I won't bother to keep asking."

I don't think this is what Jesus had in mind for us when he told us to go into all the world to make disciples. I don't think this is his plan for how to raise disciples who love him with every ounce of their being.

> **I want to love Jesus with everything I have and insist that my children join me in enjoying the adventure of following him together.**

I want my children to see the same kind of passion in me that that woman showed me that day in Serbia. I want to love Jesus with everything I have and insist that my children join me in enjoying the adventure of following him together. I don't want to take no for an answer. I want to stop them at every opportunity I get, look them in the eye, tenderly hold their precious faces in my hands, and invite them to enjoy God's goodness with me.

Because the best things in life are meant to be shared. And there is no greater news than the good news Jesus brings.

May we be so in love with Jesus that our children can't help but be in love with him as well. May we know in the deepest parts of our beings that nothing we can give to our children is better than the gospel of Jesus. And may we insist that they share in that with us.

At the end of the day, God is sovereign. The journey our children take with Jesus does not solely rest on our shoulders. They may turn down the Snickers bar, but I never stop asking them to join me. You can passionately invite your children into plenty of things, but what will last for eternity?

Do you want to raise children who love God's Word? Become a man who loves God's Word. Do you want to raise children who obey the voice of their heavenly father? Become a man who obeys the voice of his heavenly father. Do you want to raise children who seek after the treasures of the kingdom more than the treasures of this world? Become a man who longs for the things of God more than the things of this world.

> **May we be fathers who aren't just passionate about good things. May we be passionate about eternal things.**

Your kids ultimately don't need to have the best report card in their class. They don't need to excel at a sport or master an instrument. Ultimately, your kids need Jesus. May we be fathers who aren't just passionate about good things. May we be passionate about eternal things. Running toward anything else is running toward the wrong end zone.

PART 2

THE KINGDOM OF GOD IN YOU

4

THE SYRUP AISLE

Stumbling Through Spiritual Leadership
Is Better Than Doing Nothing

Our family has been trying to get into a rhythm of practicing Sabbath on Saturdays. We usually start this rest-filled day by cooking a giant batch of pancakes and enjoying a long breakfast together. The kids sit down at the table to color while Leila and I work on getting the pancakes ready. We ask Alexa to blast some worship music throughout the house, and sometimes the kitchen turns into a dance floor, where I usually look like a fool and the kids laugh at my terrible dance moves.

A few weeks ago, we slowly rolled out of bed and began our normal Sabbath routine. We cooked an obnoxious number of pancakes and all sat down, prepared to eat. Then we realized something terrible had happened...

We had run out of syrup.

Nothing is worse than trying to eat pancakes without syrup. It's like trying to eat cereal without milk. Or pizza without ranch. It's just not the way God intended things to be.

Fortunately, we live about thirty-five seconds away from Target, so Leila volunteered to quickly run to the store to rescue us from our breakfast catastrophe. The kids and I waited patiently at the table while she headed out.

Five minutes went by. And then ten. And then thirty.

The pancakes turned cold, and the kids were beyond restless. I decided to call Leila to see what was going on.

"Hey, babe, everything okay?" I asked.

"Yeah, sorry. I've been standing in the syrup aisle trying to decide which one is best for our kids. There are *so* many options…I don't want to pick the wrong one!" She was almost in a panic.

"Um, babe. Just grab one. Any one. We're starving over here."

> **When it comes to being the spiritual leader of their homes, a lot of guys suffer from analysis paralysis.**

My wife suffers from what I call "analysis paralysis." If she is presented with too many options, she freezes and can't seem to decide. She's convinced that if she doesn't know everything about everything, she may end up making the wrong decision, even about something as trivial as pancake syrup. Analysis paralysis is the inability to move forward or make a decision without first feeling like you have all the information.

Of course, it's not so much a condition as something we laugh at. Well, at least most of the time. Waiting thirty minutes to put syrup on your pancakes is no laughing matter.

When it comes to being the spiritual leader of their homes, a lot of guys also suffer from analysis paralysis. The options of what they should be doing can feel overwhelming and cause them to freeze. Instead of stumbling their way forward, they don't do anything at all.

What devotional do I choose?

What podcasts should I listen to?

Do I even know the Bible well enough to teach my kids?

What do I do if they don't sit quietly while I'm trying to teach them?

What if they can tell I don't really know what I'm talking about?

Are we supposed to listen to K-Love every day?

What's the right way to pray with my kids? And the list goes on…

Many guys think that if they move too quickly, without first analyzing all the options, they will make a mistake. And here's the truth—you probably will.

Leila could have spent years in that syrup aisle, gathering all the information she could, and still have picked the "wrong one." But we didn't need the perfect syrup. We simply needed something to dip our pancakes into while we enjoyed breakfast together as a family.

Despite your best efforts and all your research, there will always be more to learn. Because the crazy thing about God is that the more you learn, the more you realize how much you don't know. Studying God's Word doesn't lead to all the answers; usually it brings up more questions.

> **Here's one thing I've learned from watching great spiritual leaders who have gone before me: They don't overthink it. They simply read the Bible and do what it says.**

Here's one thing I've learned from watching great spiritual leaders who have gone before me: They don't overthink it. They simply read the Bible and do what it says. They aren't perfect dads or the best theologians, but they are stumbling their way forward. They are making mistakes, learning from them, and moving on.

Your family doesn't need the perfect spiritual leader, but they do need someone who will lead them toward Jesus. You can spend your whole life trying to gather more information about being the perfect spiritual leader of your home. But meanwhile, your family is sitting at the table, starving.

> **Your family doesn't need the perfect spiritual leader, but they do need someone who will lead them toward Jesus.**

Leila and I have opposite personalities. She moves painfully slow when trying to make a decision, but I move dangerously fast. I make decisions without thinking through all the consequences, and as a result, I often make dumb ones.

A few years ago, I had some wisdom teeth removed. I had procrastinated on the procedure as a teenager, and it finally caught up to me as an adult. The teeth were overcrowded, and my mouth was in a ton of pain.

When I arrived at the dentist's office, the dental assistant handed me an apron to cover my shirt during the procedure. Just a month earlier, I'd had an emergency appendectomy, so I felt comfortable with the surgery process. Without thinking too much about it, I stripped myself of all my clothes and slipped on the small apron.

When the dental assistant walked back into the room, she was in shock.

"Um, sir. You can put your pants back on. We're just going to be working on your mouth today," she said in utter disbelief of what I had done.

"Oh yeah, of course. I was just trying to prepare for the worst," I said jokingly, trying to make light of the situation.

I moved quickly, and as a result, I failed. It happens. But instead of turning it into a big situation, I simply pulled on my pants, laughed at myself, and got my wisdom teeth pulled out.

Whether you move as slow as Leila in the syrup aisle or as quickly as me at the dental office, you are bound to make mistakes along the way. The good news is that God isn't expecting you to be the perfect leader. And neither are your kids. They don't need perfection—they need initiation.

When our kids were old enough to start school, Leila and I decided to homeschool them. We found a curriculum called Classical Conversations, which is a Christian-based homeschooling program that uses the classical education model to teach children. One of my favorite things they tell the parents in the program is that we are the lead learners. This means that as our kids' parents and teachers, we aren't expected to have all the answers, but we are expected to engage in learning with our children. This gave me a ton of relief. To be honest, I was scared to death of homeschooling our kids.

There are so many options for each subject. Where do I even begin? I thought to myself. *What if I mess it up and they fail in life? What if they realize I don't even know how to do basic math?*

I'd never been a good student at school and didn't feel qualified to teach my kids. But I knew I could be the lead learner. I knew that even though I didn't know all the answers, if I was committed enough to their education, I could learn with my kids.

> **We should be the first in our families to initiate and explore what it means to fall in love with Jesus and follow in his ways.**

I think God has the same expectation for us as parents when it comes to raising disciples who look like Jesus. He knows we don't have all the answers and that we will sometimes find ourselves looking like fools with our pants down. But that isn't an excuse to not engage. As men, our job is to become lead learners of the kingdom of God. We should be the first in our families to initiate and explore what it means to fall in love with Jesus and follow in his ways.

When it comes to being the spiritual leader of my home, I like to think of myself less like an expert and more like a guide.

We live in the Pacific Northwest, so we're lucky enough to have some of the world's most beautiful scenery in our own backyard. We can be at the base of a giant waterfall or the cliffs of the ocean in less than two hours. I love to be outside and to explore the outdoors. Because of my highly spontaneous personality, I often say to my kids, "Let's go on an adventure!" We stuff a backpack full of snacks and head out to explore a trail we've never been to.

> This is what spiritual leadership should look like in our homes. We are guides toward the things of God, not necessarily experts.

As we hike, I feel like it's my job to point out all the amazing things happening around us. My kids like to move fast, and sometimes because of that, they miss the coolest parts of nature right beneath their feet. I'll often stop them to observe a giant banana slug trying to cross the trail. Or point out a waterfall peeking through the trees. Or tell them to look up at the birds nesting in the forest.

I'm no expert in banana slugs, waterfalls, or birds. I'm simply pointing out what's happening around them. In fact, I never feel the need to create amazing things when we're out exploring. I just point my kids' eyes toward the amazing things that are already there.

This is what spiritual leadership should look like in our homes. We are guides toward the things of God, not necessarily experts.

Let me give you some good news, bro: You don't have to create amazing things for your kids. Instead, point their eyes toward the amazing things God is already doing around them.

Are you willing to be a spiritual guide for your family? If so, slow down

You don't have to
create amazing things
for your kids.
Instead, point their eyes
toward the amazing
things God is already
doing around them.

enough to see what he is doing around you. If you move too fast while hiking, you miss the banana slugs at your feet. And if you move too fast in life, you miss the little things God is doing in the lives of your wife and children. It's easy for us to get into survival mode and simply power through our days. We spend long hours at work, feed the kids, make sure they are doing the right thing in school, keep the house clean, and then try to get them to bed. But if we rush through the day, we often miss what God is doing around us. A good guide slows down enough to see the little things that others might be missing. Sometimes this means you need to make sure your family slows down enough to have a meal together while you talk about the ways you see God working around you.

> **If you move too fast in life, you miss the little things God is doing in the lives of your wife and children.**

At dinner, I'll often ask my family, "What did you see God do today?"

Sometimes that leads to simple things, like admiring the sunset or watching the birds in our backyard. But other times, it leads to conversations about having to learn forgiveness with neighborhood friends or trusting God to provide for our needs when Daddy wasn't able to land a certain job at work.

At this moment, God is actively working in the lives of your wife and children. He is pursuing their hearts and turning them back to the way things were meant to be. He is working on their selfishness, their sin, their unbelief, their doubt, their fears, and their anxieties. He is taking all their brokenness and making it new. As a guide, you can point out the amazing work he is doing in them and make sure they don't miss it.

Are you willing to be a lead learner when it comes to following Jesus? If so, grab your Bible and start reading it with your kids. You won't understand everything, and they certainly won't understand everything, but you can explore it together. There are tons of resources that can help you make sense of things.[1] As you read, ask yourself, *What did I learn about God today, and how does that change the way I live?* Once you answer that, simply spend the rest of the day, week, and month practicing together what it looks like to live out what you've learned.

My kids often ask me questions about God that I don't know the answer to. It's okay to say, "That's a great question. I don't really know the answer. Let's open the Bible and see if we can find an answer together."

You don't have to be the expert. You are a guide and the lead learner.

RIGHT CONTENT, WRONG TIMING

Last year, one of the elementary schools near us put on a free community event for the kids in our neighborhood. They invited a bunch of firefighters, dentists, and local community leaders to read stories to the kids and offered free pizza and cupcakes to all the attendees. Leila had to work but insisted that I take Elijah and Eden. She had been texting me the entire day, making sure I didn't forget about the event.

When the time finally rolled around, I packed up the kids in the car and drove to the school. The parking lot was nearly empty, which was surprising because they had been promoting the event. I got the kids out of the car, and we walked to the main entrance of the school, only to find that the doors were locked. I pulled out my phone and texted Leila: "Doors are locked. Are you sure there is an event here tonight?"

"A hundred percent sure. Walk around to the back—it's probably happening outside on the field," she replied.

I walked with the kids around to the back of the school, and sure enough,

---

[1] The Bible Project is an amazing resource for helping you and your kids understand each book of the Bible. Check it out at thebibleproject.com.

we found the other parents eating pizza and cupcakes with their children. I dished up a plate for the kids and then told them to go play with their friends.

The entire time I was there, I could feel other parents staring at me. We live in a small town, and I speak at a lot of churches, so I concluded that they recognized me from a service I had taught at. I kept eating my pizza and didn't think much of it.

After several minutes of me awkwardly standing around by myself, I heard one of the parents shout out to all the kids playing in the field, "Okay, team, bring it in! Let's gather around coach as he passes out the trophies!"

My heart sank.

I immediately realized I was at the wrong place. This was not a community reading night. This was an end-of-the-year party for a soccer team, and I had just stolen about half of their pizza and cupcakes.

Now I knew why all the parents were staring at me the whole time and why no one was talking to me.

I quickly called for Eden and Elijah to come to me.

"Do you guys want to race to the car?" I whispered in their ears.

"Yes!" they shouted.

"Okay," I said softly. "One, two, three, go!"

The three of us ran to the car, and I immediately started to burst into laughter when the car doors were shut behind us. My kids had no idea what was going on, but they started laughing too.

I had just crashed a soccer party, and instead of owning up to it, I ran away with my kids.

I'm such an idiot.

Here's the lesson I learned that day: Even though the content was right, the timing was wrong. Yes, there were pizza and cupcakes and kids, but I was a week early. Leila had entered the wrong date into our calendar. And even though everything felt right, it was definitely wrong.

Right content, wrong timing.

As you stumble your way through spiritual leadership, you will find yourself in lots of situations where the content is right but the timing is wrong.

I recently took Elijah to the grocery store to grab a few things. As soon as we parked, he said, "Daddy, I have to go potty."

"Number one or number two?"

"Two," he said. Of course.

Why do kids always wait to go to the bathroom at the worst possible time? I told him that we'd be quick and that he could go when we got back to the house.

We got into the store and quickly made our way through the aisles, grabbing what we needed. As we were looking for the cereal we wanted, I could hear a couple in the aisle next to us arguing. They were uncomfortably loud, and the man was being quite rude to the woman. At one point, I heard him say, "Just know that I'll never forgive you for this."

I looked down at Elijah to see if he was listening. He looked a little scared and had clearly heard their whole conversation.

I got down on a knee and looked him straight into his eyes. Not wanting to miss an opportunity to disciple my son, I started talking to him about forgiveness.

"Son, the reason we will never stop forgiving people is that God never stops forgiving us. We can forgive with unending forgiveness because God forgives us with unending forgiveness."

To my surprise, his eyes started filling up with tears. I couldn't believe it. I had waited a long time to have this kind of spiritual breakthrough with my kids, and here it was happening at a grocery store.

Brother,
you are going
to stumble
your way
through this
whole spiritual
leadership thing.

As the tears started slowly streaming down his little cheeks, he looked at me and said, "Daddy, I really have to poopy. I think it's an emergency."

He hadn't heard a word of my little sermon. He was in the middle of a bathroom emergency.

The content was right. The timing was wrong.

Remember the story of Joseph in Genesis 37? Joseph is the son of Jacob (Israel) and has a bunch of older brothers. One day he has a dream that all his older brothers will one day bow down to him. Being his dad's favorite son, Joseph already isn't very liked by his brothers, but this takes their animosity to a whole new level. They are so mad at him that they plot to kill him but sell him as a slave instead.

Or what about the story of Peter and Jesus rebuking each other? Jesus teaches his disciples that he will be arrested, beaten, and killed. This doesn't sit well with Peter. The Bible says that Peter takes Jesus aside to have a little chat. He explains that Jesus is wrong and that these things will never happen to him. Needless to say, the talk doesn't go very well, and Jesus ends up calling Peter "Satan." It was a bad day for Peter.

In both these stories, the content was good, but the timing was wrong.

I had the right heart when trying to disciple Elijah in the grocery store. Joseph had the right heart when trying to tell his brothers about his dream from God. And Peter had the right heart when trying to tell Jesus that he didn't want him to die. But we all failed. Even with the best intentions, we failed.

The cool thing about following Christ is that God can use even our failures for his glory.

Joseph was sold into slavery but eventually found himself right where God wanted him. He went on to become the God-fearing leader of a nation. Peter heard some hard words from Jesus that day but eventually emerged as a key leader in the advancement of Christianity and the early church.

At the grocery store, I found myself slightly embarrassed as my little teachable moment flew straight over my son's head. But God, by his grace, will take my stumbling and use it for his glory. My goal is to eventually hear my son say, "My daddy loved Jesus and used every opportunity to tell me more about him."

> **God isn't looking for perfection—he is looking for initiation.**

Brother, you are going to stumble your way through this whole spiritual leadership thing. You will likely find yourself embarrassed, incapable, and incompetent. Don't let that stop you from moving forward. God isn't looking for perfection—he is looking for initiation. Have the courage to initiate your family in the things of God. Be a guide who points out the work God is already doing around them. God will honor your effort and use it for his glory. Even your failures can be used to advance his kingdom.

LIFE IS BUT A MIST

A few weeks ago, Leila and I were enjoying a cup of coffee in the backyard as she was telling me some recent stories from her work. She has worked at the local hospital as an oncology nurse, caring for cancer patients, for the past eleven years. Leila has the honor of walking people through some of the hardest and scariest seasons of their lives. For many of these patients, these seasons will end in death.

As we sat in the backyard, Leila was telling me about a young father who found out he had terminal cancer. He had two kids under the age of ten and had felt no prior symptoms of sickness. He had been fixing a leak in the roof when he slipped off and fell to the ground, breaking several ribs. An X-ray of his chest revealed a large mass, and his doctors realized he had a much bigger problem than a couple of broken ribs. He was likely going to die in the near future.

My heart broke.

I couldn't imagine the emotional pain that he, his wife, and their children would be experiencing in the coming months. For him, what started out as a normal day, making some repairs around the house, turned into his worst nightmare. He would spend his final days on earth saying goodbye to the ones who mattered most.

We sat on the back patio in silence awhile, taking in the heaviness of this family's new reality. After several minutes, these words slipped out of my mouth: "I feel like I will have a similar story."

"Really?" Leila said, surprised by what I had just said.

Honestly, I too was slightly surprised by my own words. I didn't expect to say something so heavy and almost morbid.

Maybe I have thoughts like these because my wife works as an oncology nurse and shares cancer stories with me on a regular basis. Or maybe I just have a twisted brain. But something inside me is convinced that I, too, will lose my life to cancer at a young age.

Don't get me wrong—I have no desire to die. Everything in me wants to live a long life for the glory of God. But something in my gut tells me that I will be one of those statistics and that I, too, will find myself in an office similar to the one where Leila works, hearing words that will mark the beginning of my end.

I think about this reality on a regular basis.

Just yesterday I did a FaceTime call with my mom to catch up on what was going on in her life. In a couple of months, I'll be taking her on a cruise with my family as kind of a belated thank-you for putting up with me for all those years. I asked her if she wanted to swim with some stingrays while we visit a tropical island in the Caribbean.

She instantly replied, "No way! Those things can kill you!" We both laughed.

"What about trying some local Mexican food from a street vendor?" I asked.

"Are you kidding me? I don't want to spend the rest of my vacation sick in the bathroom."

"Mom," I said, this time with a more serious tone, "if I beat all the odds and somehow live until I'm ninety years old, that means I only have fifty-nine years left on this earth. Fifty. Nine. Years. Think about how quickly a year goes by. In the best-case scenario, I'd only have fifty-nine left. Life is too short. We have to start taking more risks in life."

> **Death has a powerful way of reminding us of what really matters.**

I could see tears start to fill her eyes. The week before our call, her aunt had passed away, and I knew this topic was hitting a nerve.

"I've been thinking about that a lot lately, son. And you're right. Life is too short. Let's eat some street tacos. But I'm still not swimming with stingrays!" she said through a small laugh as she wiped the tears from her eyes.

Death has a powerful way of reminding us of what really matters. It's why Jesus's brother James says,

> Now listen, you who say, "Today or tomorrow we will go to this or that city, spend a year there, carry on business and make money." Why, you do not even know what will happen tomorrow. What is your life? You are a mist that appears for a little while and then vanishes" (James 4:13-14 NIV).

If we're not careful, we can start to convince ourselves that we have plenty of time to figure out this whole spiritual leadership thing. We subconsciously slip into the mindset that our kids will be young forever, that we'll always have an opportunity to influence them, and that we never really have to think about death.

Brother, your life is a mist. Even if you somehow beat all the odds and live an incredibly long life, you still have very little time. Think about how quickly this last year flew by. Think about how fast your kids are growing up or how long you've already been married. And somehow the older we get, the faster the years seem to speed along.

When it comes to being the spiritual leader of your family, you don't have the luxury of standing paralyzed in the syrup aisle while your family waits for your return. Yes, there are an overwhelming number of ways you can start to engage. Yes, you will find yourself with your pants down at the dentist's office because you made a decision too fast. Yes, you will find your-

A spiritual leader knows it's better to stumble his way through than to make no effort at all.

self giving your kids the best sermon of your life, only to see them giving you the most confused blank stare in return. You will fail. You will fall short. But by God's grace, he will use you to draw your family a little closer to his heart.

Don't wait another day to figure out all the answers. You are simply a guide. The amazing God of the universe has already done incredible things around you—simply point them out. He is already working to draw the hearts of your wife and kids back to himself, so have the courage to slow down and join him in that beautiful work of redemption.

A spiritual leader knows it's better to stumble his way through than to make no effort at all. Life is too short. Grab the syrup—any syrup—run home, and start digging in.

5

HIDE-AND-SEEK

Don't Let Sin and Shame Stop You from Leading Your Family

When my nephews were young, I used to spend hours playing hide-and-seek with them in our house. I'm not sure who enjoyed it more, me or them. During one of our countless games together, I told four-year-old Nathaniel that I would count to twenty as he went to find his best hiding place. I finished my counting and then started my hunt throughout the house. After searching all the bedrooms with no luck, I made my way into the living room. Nathaniel was standing in the middle of the room with his eyes closed. He was in plain sight, with nothing around him, totally convinced that because he couldn't see me, I couldn't see him. I laughed at how cute it was to watch this little guy try to figure out what it means to hide well.

When Nathaniel was four, he wasn't very good at hide-and-seek. But it didn't take long for him to figure out how to hide well.

Let's revisit Adam and Eve in the garden. Despite having everything they needed to live a fulfilled life, they decided their ways were better than God's ways. They believed Satan's lie that they needed something other than God to satisfy their souls. As a result, they turned their backs on God. After taking the fruit and eating it, they hid themselves from God among the trees.

In their shame, they hid.

Growing up, my friends and I constantly looked for ways to keep ourselves entertained during the long California summers. We didn't have cell phones and couldn't afford video games, so we were forced to go outside and look for creative ways to stay busy. Those are some of my fondest childhood memories. Even now as a dad, I let my kids face boredom so they'll use their own creativity to go outside and find something fun to do.

One boring summer day, my friends and I decided to rummage through the garage to see what we could find. Behind some old paint cans and motor oil, we stumbled upon an old rusty chain.

"We could build a swing in the tree!" I said enthusiastically.

My friends agreed to the idea, and we quickly got to work.

Using the best engineering our ten-year-old brains could muster, we spent the next several hours constructing a swing high in the branches of an old walnut tree in my backyard. Using a ladder, we were able to assemble a seat ten feet above the ground. As we finished, we took a minute to pause and soak in the beauty of our handiwork. We soon realized that none of us had the courage to take the first ride and that we would need a younger neighborhood kid to be the crash test dummy for us.

After a bit of bribery and a lot of peer pressure, we were able to convince one of the younger brothers to be the first to try the swing. We were all smiles as we helped him climb on and slowly twisted the swing, knotting up the chain. After about twenty or thirty twists, we told him we were going to let go of the swing so he could enjoy spinning around.

Then we let go.

For the first few seconds, we were having the time of our lives. The swing was working exactly as we had designed it to, and we were quite impressed with ourselves.

And then the chain snapped.

The giant smiles on our faces fell as fast as the younger brother fell, his body parallel to the ground.

Thump! He landed hard at my feet.

I could see him fight to gasp for air, but the wind was knocked out of him. He hit the ground hard and couldn't catch his breath. I still remember the look of panic on his face as he desperately fought for air. It absolutely terrified me.

Being the oldest of all the friends, I knew I needed to do something. So I did what any other ten-year-old boy would do in that situation. I ran.

I ran as fast as I could into the house and locked every door behind me. I hid under my bed and cried for hours, knowing the kind of trouble I would be in when my mom got home from work.

> **We've never stopped hiding. We've been hiding since the beginning of creation.**

To this day, I have no idea what happened to my friend's younger brother who fell off the swing.

WE'RE STILL HIDING

In the Garden of Eden, Adam and Eve were convinced that if God really knew them and all they had done, he wouldn't want to be around them. So they hid.

The thing is, I don't think we've ever stopped hiding as humans. We've been hiding since the beginning of creation.

Adam and Eve hid in the garden, afraid that their sin would be exposed.

As a boy, I hid under my bed, fearful that my mistakes would be the end of me.

My seven-year-old son hides his face in shame when he knows he's treated his sister wrongly.

And as adults, we don't stop hiding—we just get more creative. Instead of standing in the middle of the living room with our eyes closed, we've found better ways to cover ourselves. Instead of hiding under our beds or behind some trees in the garden, we find other ways to mask ourselves.

Like with fancy job titles.

Or big bank accounts.

Or nice cars.

Or strong opinions on Facebook.

Or jokes.

Or success at work.

Or video games.

Or fantasy football.

Or polished Instagram accounts.

Or pithy Twitter updates.

We've become experts in hiding, convinced that if God and the rest of the world really knew us, they'd want nothing to do with us. For many guys, the heaviness of their sin and shame have become too much to bear, so they do what humans have always done—they hide.

In chapter 4, I talked about men getting paralyzed by not knowing what it looks like to be the spiritual leaders of their families. Many guys didn't have an example of what that leadership looks like practically, and as a result, they end up not doing anything because they simply don't know where to begin.

There are many guys, however, who are struggling with something entirely different. They know exactly how they could be engaging their family on a spiritual level. They aren't paralyzed by the number of options there are, but instead, they are paralyzed by their own sin and shame. They are convinced that leading their families toward Jesus would mean that they too must draw close to Jesus, and as a result, they may have to deal with their own brokenness. And for many, that weight is too heavy to consider bearing.

Maybe you, like Adam and Eve in the garden, are convinced that if God really knew you and all that you had done, he would want nothing to do with you. Maybe you're buried by the weight of your sin and shame. Maybe you're convinced that it would be better to continue hiding than to draw close to Jesus and risk being exposed. Maybe you've been absent as the spiritual leader of your home because you don't quite have your own life figured out, and you can't imagine leading your family close to a God that you currently feel far from.

> **Maybe you, like Adam and Eve in the garden, are convinced that if God really knew you and all that you had done, he would want nothing to do with you.**

Brother, if that's you, I have good news.

GOD WITH US

Do you remember what God was doing on one of the worst days in human history? As Adam and Eve were busy hiding from God in their shame, God was taking a walk. He wasn't screaming. He wasn't destroying the world. He wasn't starting over with a new humanity. He was walking with these two sinful, broken people. He was right there in their midst—not correcting from afar but engaging in their presence.

This is the reputation of the God of the Bible. He is always among broken and messy people.

In the book of Exodus, we see the Israelites, God's chosen people, rebelling against the God who miraculously rescued them from Egypt. They were once slaves under Pharaoh, but by God's grace, they were set free from slavery and were making their way to a better land. Time after time God had shown up to provide for them, rescue them, and comfort them along their journey.

> **This is the reputation of the God of the Bible. He is always among broken and messy people.**

And how do they respond? By complaining. In fact, some of the Israelites say they would rather return as slaves in Egypt than continue wandering in the desert. They grow angry and bitter toward God and question his goodness. On one occasion, they even construct a golden idol in the image of a cow. They are far from God and disobedient to him. They have turned their hearts away from him.

And what does God do in the middle of their sin and brokenness? He sticks around. Listen to what he says to them in their moment of wandering and confusion: "Let them make me a sanctuary, that I may dwell in their midst" (Exodus 25:8).

This is crazy.

The holy and perfect God—the Creator of the universe, who has every right to bail on the people who have turned their backs on him—says he wants to dwell in their midst. He doesn't want a long-distance relationship. He doesn't say he'll check in on them from time to time when they get their act together. He doesn't tell them to shape up or he's going to leave them to themselves. Instead, he tells them that in the middle of their sin, their brokenness, even their evil, he wants to dwell among them.

God has a reputation for wanting to be near broken and messy people.

But this isn't the end of the story; he takes it one step further. God, the author of this grand story of redemption, decides to enter into his own story in flesh and blood. I love the way the Gospel of Matthew says, "'Behold, the virgin shall conceive and bear a son, and they shall call his name Immanuel' (which means, God with us)" (1:23).

The God of the Bible is the God who walked with sinful people in the garden.

He's the God who dwelled with sinful people in the desert.

And he's the God who put on the clothing of humanity and walked on the earth with broken and sinful people.

God is *with* us.

He's not a god who is far off in the distance. Or a god who shouts. Or a god who checks in on his people from time to time. He's Immanuel, the God who is with us—the God who has a reputation for being near broken and messy people.

Imagine Jesus treating people the way we think he would treat us because of our sin. The New Testament would be full of stories of him pushing broken people aside and giving preference to those who had their act together.

Instead, we see quite the opposite.

In fact, the people who seemed to have their act together, the religious leaders, had nicknames for Jesus. They called him "a glutton and a drunkard" and "a friend of tax collectors and sinners" (Matthew 11:19).

> God has a reputation for wanting to be near broken and messy people.

Jesus had a reputation among the religious folk for wanting to be near the sinners, the broken, and the people who didn't have it all figured out.

That's good news.

If you were considered a religious outsider in Jesus's day, you would have felt comfortable having a meal with him. If you felt burdened by guilt and shame from your mistakes, you would have felt safe around him. If you felt like you didn't really belong around the people who had their lives in order, you would have found peace in the person and message of Jesus.

Jesus was not only around broken people; he was also their friend. He liked them and they liked him.

This is why it would have been a punch in the disciples' gut to hear Jesus say he was going to die on a cross and leave them. It would have shattered their spirits.

They had waited hundreds of years for the Messiah to show up and rescue them. And finally, here he was, in flesh and blood. They were walking around with the God of all creation. They were able to have him over for dinner, share meals together, pick his brain, ask his opinion, and hear his honest thoughts.

This is the God of the universe we're talking about! And he's their friend!

You would be angry too if you got to always hang around the God of the universe, and then suddenly he said he was leaving.

I would have probably done the same thing Peter did when he pulled Jesus aside and basically said, "Nah, man. You can't leave."

But the truth is, he didn't leave. Listen to what Jesus tells his friends in John:

> I will ask the Father, and he will give you another helper who will be with you forever. That helper is the Spirit of Truth. The world cannot accept him, because it doesn't see or know him. You know him, because he lives with you and will be in you.
>
> I will not leave you all alone. I will come back to you. In a little while the world will no longer see me, but you will see me. You will live because I live. On that day you will know that I am in my Father and that you are in me and that I am in you (John 14:16-20 GW).

Catch this: The God who walked with Adam and Eve after they sinned in the garden is the same God who dwelled among the rebellious Israelites in the desert. He's the same God who put on flesh and blood and entered a broken and sinful world in the person of Jesus. And now God is saying he doesn't just want to dwell *among* them but wants to dwell *in* them.

Now, to us that may not sound like that big of a deal, but to his disciples, that would have been revolutionary. The spirit of the holy and perfect God dwelling *in* them? No way.

They were too broken. Too messy. Too sinful.

Being students of the Scriptures, they would have known that God dwells only in the most holy of temples. In fact, they would have known that the presence of God was so holy and powerful that if anyone other than the high priest entered the Most Holy Place (and even he could enter it only once a year), that person could lose his life. Entering the temple where God's presence dwelled was reserved only for those who were chosen by God and who had been made clean through ceremonial cleansing.

God's presence was powerful and would not have been taken lightly.

Yet Jesus tells them that he is going to put his own Spirit inside of them. No longer would they have to find God walking in the garden or dwelling in a temple. They would now become the temple, the dwelling place for the most holy God.

Keep in mind that Jesus wasn't talking to perfectly sinless people. He was talking to his disciples, who were full of brokenness. They weren't high priests. They hadn't gone through a ceremonial cleansing process.

Jesus would receive them in their brokenness and make them clean. He was going to make them worthy of being a temple where his Spirit could reside. He was going to live in them—not because they had done something amazing or worked extra hard to earn his favor, but because he was about to do something amazing on their behalf.

This is what Jesus means when he says, "Whoever has seen me has seen the Father" (John 14:9).

If you were
considered a religious
outsider in
Jesus's day, you
would have felt
comfortable having
a meal with him.

God the Father has a reputation for wanting to be near broken and messy people.

Jesus has a reputation for being near broken and messy people.

The Spirit has a reputation for living in people who were once broken and messy.

BREAKFAST IS READY

In case you're not convinced and still believe that you're the one person on earth God wouldn't want to be around, let me remind you of a story from my favorite guy in the Bible, Peter.

Some would argue that Peter and Jesus were best friends. They did practically everything together. Out of the twelve disciples who walked with Jesus every day for three years, Peter was one of only three disciples who experienced some of the most intimate and unique moments with him.

The Bible uses the Greek term *emblepo* to describe Jesus's first interaction with Peter (John 1:42). This word gives readers the idea that it was more than a casual introduction with a simple handshake. In fact, handshakes wouldn't have been the norm back then. *Emblepo* is a term that describes the way that they looked each other in the eyes. It's the kind of look you give people when you have an instant connection with them, almost as if you're looking past their eyes and deep into their souls.

That connection would only grow deeper as the two spent three and a half years of daily ministry together.

We know from the Bible that Jesus lived with Peter for a time. They were housemates. They ate tons of meals together and undoubtedly shared many laughs. And we all remember the famous story of Jesus calling Peter out of his boat to miraculously walk with him on the water (Matthew 14). This was a friend inviting another friend to join him in the unthinkable. Jesus believed that Peter could experience a little bit of heaven on earth and gave him a glimpse of how things were supposed to be.

On one occasion, Peter publicly declares Jesus as God. He has the courage and tenacity to say in front of his friends that Jesus isn't just a best friend—he's also the Creator of all things. Jesus goes on to commend Peter and tell the crowd that the entire church would be built on Peter's statement of faith (see Matthew 16:16-18).

To say Peter and Jesus were just close friends would be a massive understatement. They shared the deepest parts of their lives together. They were willing to die for each other.

That's why it's no surprise on the night Jesus gets arrested that Peter pulls out his sword to defend the friend he loves so dearly. He takes a swing at the head of a soldier, doing whatever it takes to make sure Jesus will be safe (see John 18:10).

Despite his efforts, he misses the soldier's neck and ends up chopping off the man's ear (which Jesus soon heals). Jesus is arrested and led to the unfair trial that would lead to his crucifixion.

Peter would have been absolutely devastated.

His best friend, his Savior, his partner in ministry had just been taken into custody. This is not the way Peter thought the story would end.

And then the story takes an interesting turn.

As Jesus is in the middle of his impromptu trial, a little girl comes up to Peter outside the courtroom and accuses him of being friends with Jesus, to which he replies, "I don't know him."

Wait a second.

The guy who just whipped out his sword and was willing to kill for Jesus hours earlier is now saying he doesn't know him—to a young girl?

It gets even weirder.

Within minutes, Peter is accused three times of being Jesus's disciple, and all three times he claims that he doesn't even know him.

On Peter's third denial of Jesus, the heaviness of the situation really sets in. Listen to how Luke describes it in his Gospel: "The Lord turned and looked at Peter. And Peter remembered the saying of the Lord, how he had said to him, 'Before the rooster crows today, you will deny me three times'" (Luke 22:61).

The Greek word translated "looked" is *emblepo*.

After three years of friendship, ministry, risk, and miracles, Peter claims he doesn't even know Jesus. In that very moment, Jesus looks him in the eyes just as he had when they first met.

Imagine that scenario for a minute. It's one thing to sin when you think no one is watching, but turning your back on God as he is looking you in the eye—that's something else altogether.

You'd think that Jesus would have called it quits right then and there. If even Peter can't get this whole "following Jesus" thing right, who can? Jesus poured his blood, sweat, and tears into this guy, only to have him deny him at his most vulnerable moment. I'm surprised Jesus didn't call on the angels of heaven to immediately destroy the place. That's what I would have done.

But Jesus doesn't bail on Peter. In fact, he looks him in the eyes and then continues to humbly submit himself to the authorities who are wrongly accusing him.

This puts new meaning into this famous verse: "God shows his love for us in that while we were still sinners, Christ died for us" (Romans 5:8).

While Peter was denying Christ, Jesus was preparing to die for him.

And that's exactly what he would go on to do. He would be tried unfairly, beaten, spit on, mocked, and eventually nailed on a cross.

Imagine how Peter would have felt. His last moments with Jesus, his best friend, were undoubtedly the worst moments of his life. He betrayed the one he loved and promised to never turn his back on. He didn't get a chance to say he was sorry. He didn't get a do-over to prove his loyalty.

Instead, he is left with the haunting memories of his unfaithfulness to Jesus.

I can't imagine the shame that would have kept him up at night.

> **That's who God is—always wanting to be near broken and messy people.**

Peter ends up quitting the ministry and going back to what he does best—fishing. When Peter and Jesus first met, Jesus invited him to put down his fishing nets and instead go fishing for men. But now, after three years of "man fishing," Peter is back to fishing for fish. He returns to his old way of life, doing the only thing he feels confident doing.

Several days after Jesus's death, Peter and his friends go fishing all night but with no luck. Just as the day is starting to break, they see a man standing on the shore. John yells to Peter, "It is the Lord!" When Peter hears that Jesus is alive, he jumps out of the boat and begins to swim a hundred yards to the shore to meet Jesus (see John 21).

Honestly, every time I read this story, I'm amazed by Peter's reaction. Keep in mind that the last time these two friends interacted, Peter claimed he didn't even know Jesus.

If I had just denied Jesus, you wouldn't find me jumping out of the boat and swimming toward him. Instead, you'd probably find me hiding under a blanket and asking my friends to row the boat in the opposite direction.

Because that's what we do when we sin. We hide. We convince ourselves that if God really knew us and everything we had done, he would never want to be around us.

But Peter must have known something about Jesus that I'm still trying to grasp. He knew that Jesus doesn't rub sin in the face of the sinful. He doesn't hold grudges. He doesn't push people aside when they don't have their lives together.

Jesus isn't like your boss.

He isn't your wife.

He isn't your dad.

He isn't the friend who turned his back on you.

No, Peter knew that Jesus, like his Father, was "merciful and gracious, slow to anger, and abounding in steadfast love and faithfulness, keeping steadfast love for thousands, forgiving iniquity and transgression and sin" (Exodus 34:6-7).

And Peter was right.

When he finally got to shore, soaking wet, he found Jesus had been cooking him breakfast.

That's right. Jesus had breakfast ready for Peter. He was inviting him back to the table.

Because that's who God is—always wanting to be near broken and messy people.

> **Rest assured, you are thinking about your past a lot more than Jesus is.**

He is near Adam and Eve in the garden.

He is near the Israelites in the desert.

He is near his followers in flesh and blood.

He is near in his believers through his Spirit living inside of them.

He is near Peter even when Peter is at his worst.

And brother, he wants to be near you. Even at your worst.

This isn't a fluffy "Jesus loves you" pep talk. It's the gospel. It's the good news for all who believe.

God didn't wait for any of those people to be perfect before drawing near to them. And he's not waiting for you to be perfect to draw near to you. Jesus is walking near you in the garden. He's dwelling with you in the desert. He's living inside of you. He's cooking you breakfast after your worst mistake. He's searching the whole house, checking under every bed, longing to be near you.

Perhaps you're afraid of what it would look like to lead your family toward Jesus because if you did, it might force you out of hiding. But I want to remind you of two things.

First, 1 John 1:9 tells us, "If we confess our sins, he is faithful and just to forgive us our sins and to cleanse us from all unrighteousness."

> **You don't need forgiveness; you are already forgiven. Instead, you need healing.**

You aren't dealing with a grumpy God. You are dealing with the God of the Bible—one who is known for his radical grace and mercy. It's not that he overlooks sins, but even better, he punishes them once and for all. The good news is that that punishment was put on Jesus, not on you.

So you don't have to walk around in shame with your head held low. You can walk in confidence that God is who he says he is in his word. If he says he will forgive you, then you are forgiven. Period.

Rest assured, you are thinking about your past a lot more than Jesus is.

And second, you may have confessed your sin to God countless times and yet still seem unable to shake your guilt and shame. You may believe that God has forgiven you, but you walk around with a heaviness that won't go away. You are forgiven, but you aren't healed.

This is why James says, "Therefore, confess your sins to one another and pray for one another, that you may be healed. The prayer of a righteous person has great power as it is working" (James 5:16).

You don't need forgiveness; you are already forgiven. Instead, you need healing.

I can't encourage you highly enough to find a brother whom you trust and to regularly confess your sins to each other. This isn't so you can have some mediatory accountability partner who checks in on your behavior. It's much deeper than that. This is not a behavioral problem—this is a heart problem.

We must constantly confess our sins to one another, not just for accountability but for healing.

In order to lead your family well, you must be healed. And the good news is that God isn't eager to offer you his punishment. He has already taken care of that through Jesus. Instead, you will find a God who is eager to offer you his healing.

I invite you to step into that healing, bro.

Do you know what Paul says will lead us to repentance in Romans 2?

It's not wrath.

It's not anger.

It's not guilt or shame.

Paul says that it's God's kindness that leads us to repentance.

His kindness.

It's why the writer of Psalm 32 says, "You are a hiding place for me; you preserve me from trouble; you surround me with shouts of deliverance" (verse 7).

> **We must constantly confess our sins to one another, not just for accountability but for healing.**

When I was a little kid, I would run and hide under the bed because of my shame. The truth is, I think we're all still little boys who are hiding in our shame. Jesus would probably tell us, "You don't have to hide anymore. I'll be your hiding place."

Brother, don't let your sin and shame stop you from leading your family. They need you to point them toward Jesus in a real way. They need a broken man who is being healed by a gracious God to point them back to that heal-ing when they, too, fall short. You can't give what you don't have, and you can't teach what you haven't experienced. Come out from under the bed. Jump out of the boat and swim to Jesus. He has breakfast ready for you.

A NOTE TO YOUR WIFE

I've met countless men through the Dad Tired ministry who tell me that they have no problem confessing sin to Jesus, but they're worried about their wives' responses. They know that God will forgive them, but they aren't sure their wives can move past the pain of their shortcomings.

Listen, I know as men we can cause deep hurt. I have wounded my wife deeply in more ways than I care to think about. But this is what I was talk-ing about in chapter 2.

Your husband is going to hurt you—there is no getting around that. He will cause you pain like no one else on this earth can. And this is where you can point him, your children, and the people around you back to the gospel.

The good news of Jesus is that he demonstrates unending forgiveness, which in turn allows you to extend that same kind of grace toward your hus-band. I am not saying you should turn a blind eye toward sin or simply brush off deep hurts. But I am saying that your role in marriage is to point each other back to that amazing grace and good news.

Go to counseling if needed, talk to a pastor, or invite an older couple to walk through life with you. Do whatever it takes to move toward forgive-ness and healing. One of the greatest gifts you can give your husband is the freedom to constantly confess his sin to you and to remind him that even in his brokenness, you will not leave.

6

SQUIRREL FOOD

Look for Adventure in the Kingdom, Not in This World

As I begin writing this chapter, I'm sitting in an old hotel room in the middle of Egypt. I'm about four hours from Cairo, the capital, and can hear the hustle and bustle of the streets below my room. When I arrived in the country a week ago, we were told that any American group coming to visit Egypt must have a police escort with them at all times. Apparently, the two governments made an agreement years ago that required Egypt to provide American groups with constant police escorts. This sounds great in theory, but nothing makes tourists stick out more than having armed police officers following their every step. If we want to drive somewhere, they lead the way. If we want to shop for souvenirs in the market, they walk around next to us. They are always near.

Tonight, however, I found a way to ditch them.

Every time I travel, Leila makes me promise to bring her home some kind of local food—specifically, sweets. She doesn't care about mugs, magnets, or trinkets I could find on eBay. She wants the sweet stuff. Whenever I leave the country while she stays with the kids, I am required to bring home treats that can be found only in that country. When I get home, we sit down at the kitchen table, brew a pot of coffee or tea, and enjoy the treats together as I tell her all about the trip. Sometimes she goes on medical mission trips while I stay home with the kids, and the roles are reversed. We collect cookies, not things.

On this trip, I may have gone a little overboard on the Egyptian sweets. The Egyptians make some amazing food, including desserts, and I've purchased more boxes of goodies than my luggage can hold. So instead of checking my heart regarding my shopping habits, I've decided I would rather check an extra piece of luggage instead—a piece of luggage filled with goodies for my wife.

The problem is, I didn't have an extra piece of luggage, and I didn't want to have a police officer escort me through town as I tried to explain to him why having another suitcase is so imperative.

So I ditched the police.

I went down to the lobby where there was free Wi-Fi and pretended to check my phone, waiting for my opportunity to sneak past the police and out of the hotel. To my surprise, after only a few minutes, fifteen or twenty locals came down the stairs and started to make their way toward the door. They looked as if they had just come from a wedding celebration. Without hesitating, I lowered my baseball cap to cover my face and quietly made my way to the back of the crowd, blending in as best I could. I looked down toward the ground and held my breath as our entire group passed the police officers standing in front of the building.

I thought for sure I would be singled out and pulled aside. I was the only American in the group and the only one not wearing wedding attire. But to my surprise, I made it past the officers without them saying a word. I walked about a hundred feet from the hotel and realized I was totally free. It was just after 11:00 p.m., and the streets were still full of life. I was so excited to start exploring this new city on my own.

I began walking up and down the small roads when something struck me. Everyone, and I mean *everyone,* was watching me. I'd like to believe I can blend in with the dark-skinned crowd, but apparently I stuck out like a sore thumb. For the first time on the trip, I wished the police escorts were with me. I felt incredibly vulnerable as I walked in and out of each store, looking for a new suitcase. What if I got lost and couldn't find my way back to the hotel room? What if a group of guys decided to mug me? What if I *did* find a suitcase—was I going to walk around the Egyptian city streets at midnight rolling around a suitcase full of cookies?

What in the world was I thinking to sneak out in a foreign country on my own?

My heart was racing. I could feel my body temperature rising as all the Egyptian eyes were staring at me. It was an absolute adrenaline rush. And despite being totally freaked out, I was loving every minute of it. As small and pathetic as this task was, it turned out to be a fun little adventure.

I eventually found a little shop that happened to sell used backpacks. I figured filling up a couple of backpacks with goodies might be more practical than finding a giant suitcase.

The truth is, I don't think I was really looking for a suitcase that night. I think I was looking for an adventure. Deep down, I knew that sneaking out of the hotel, running around the streets alone, and being somewhat vulnerable would satisfy an itch for me.

Though my hunt for a suitcase may have been insignificant in the grand scheme of things, it was still an adventure. And yes, it satisfied a small part of my soul.

BORED TO TEARS

Humans love adventure. You don't have to be a scientific researcher to know that kids are born to explore and look for fun in every possible opportunity. I often work from a big comfy chair in my living room that looks out the window into my front yard. I watch as my kids and their friends find creative ways to play in the giant maple tree at the edge of our lawn. Sometimes they are sailors, trying to escape from evil pirates. Other times they are birds, building a nest in the tree. And sometimes I watch them work together to build a giant rope swing in its branches.[1]

> **Have you lost the appetite for adventure that you once had as a child and young adult? Or are you looking for it in other places?**

In the creative hands of a child, every tree, stick, and rock can be used for a new adventure.

When do we grow out of that? Do we ever really grow out of it?

When we are children, we use the raw materials of the world around us to create new adventures. When we are teenagers, we find adventures in our first dates, our first kisses, or our new driver's licenses. As college students, we find adventure in moving to a new place, making new friends, and exploring new freedoms as young adults. In our twenties, we find adventure in landing our first real jobs or getting married to the women of our dreams. In our late twenties and early thirties, we experience the rush of buying our first homes or maybe becoming fathers for the first time.

And then what?

By the world's standards, you've done everything you're supposed to do. You finished school. You got the job. You married the girl. You bought the

---

[1] This still brings back terrible memories of my rope-swing-in-the-tree days.

house. You had the kids. What is left to do? Pay bills, coach little league, and wait for the adventure of retirement to show up in thirty years?

Have you lost the appetite for adventure that you once had as a child and young adult? Or are you looking for it in other places?

I don't think men have outgrown their sense of adventure. Instead, I think they have become bored and begin looking for it elsewhere. The scary part is, a bored man is a dangerous man.

When I was on a church pastoral staff, I sometimes noticed that many of the men who showed up on Sunday morning looked depressed. Their wives wore big smiles and pretty dresses and seemed to almost drag the husbands into the building. The men walked around with stiff faces and talked about the football games they had to miss to be at church.

> **I don't think men have outgrown their sense of adventure. Instead, I think they have become bored and begin looking for it elsewhere. The scary part is, a bored man is a dangerous man.**

Honestly, I was right there with them. If I wasn't getting paid to attend church, I probably wouldn't have been there every week either. In fact, I've been guilty of checking my fantasy football scores in the middle of a sermon.

The real superheroes of the church community were the guys who volunteered their time to serve. They'd offer to greet guests and new visitors on Sunday mornings or maybe pass the offering basket in the middle of the service. If they wanted extra credit, some guys would even volunteer to host a Bible study or weekly community group in their homes.

Part of my job at the church was to encourage guys to step up and serve in these ways. It almost felt like I was trying to sell them on something they clearly didn't want to buy. When they said yes, they often seemed to do so out of obligation. I sometimes thought, *Is this really what adventure looks like for a man in the kingdom of God? There must be more to it than this.*

If I weren't a Christian and walked into an American church on a Sunday morning, outside of the Holy Spirit miraculously saving me (which I fully believe he can do), I'm not sure I'd buy into the adventure the church was selling.

> **Is this really what adventure looks like for a man in the kingdom of God? There must be more to it than this.**

Some studies seem to indicate that Christian men and the secular community are no different when it comes to addiction to pornography, adultery, divorce, and substance abuse. Honestly, I'm not really surprised. I think Satan hijacks our God-given desire for adventure and points it toward evil. He knows our hearts want more, and he wants us to find it outside of Christ.

Don't forget, this is the same deceiver from the Garden of Eden who convinced Adam and Eve they could find adventure outside of God.

Our churches are filled with bored men. Men whose souls long for adventure. Men who desire to take risks, step out in faith, and put themselves in situations where they might fail.

And how do we channel the longing burning in them?

We ask them to pass the communion trays or volunteer to vacuum the sanctuary.

No wonder our guys are searching for adventure through porn, affairs, or video games. Their hearts want more.

Please hear me loud and clear: I am not justifying any man's choice to follow his desire into sin. I am not excusing his lack of righteousness. I am

Our churches are filled
with bored men.
Men whose souls long for adventure.
Men who desire to take risks,
step out in faith, and
put themselves
in situations where
they might fail.

convinced that the Holy Spirit, God in us, can transform our hearts to live righteous lives for his glory. Rather, I am saying that church leaders (including me!) have done a terrible job of helping men fulfill their longing for adventure through service in the kingdom.

When a man comes to me to confess his addictions or his entanglement with sin, I can't help but wonder how bored he is. I often see a man who desires to live a life of adventure, but instead of finding it in Jesus, he has turned to lesser things.

LEFTOVERS

At our house, we don't own any pets—not because we don't love animals, but because we are renting a home, and our agreement says we aren't allowed to have animals in the house. My kids constantly ask me to buy them a puppy, and I always remind them that it simply isn't an option for us right now.

> I often see a man who desires to live a life of adventure, but instead of finding it in Jesus, he has turned to lesser things.

As a compromise, I have channeled my inner Ace Ventura and turned my backyard into a miniature wildlife refuge. I can hardly count all our bird feeders, bird baths, bird houses, squirrel feeders, and much more. I should charge the neighbors admission into my homemade zoo when they come over. If you were to sit down at our kitchen table for a meal, you would most likely see dozens of creatures enjoying their food just outside the sliding glass door.

The other day I was eating lunch in the kitchen when I watched a new squirrel wander into our backyard. And yes, I knew it was a new squirrel because we have identified and named each animal that comes onto our property. I hadn't seen this little guy before.

He climbed our fence and scrambled along the top. I could tell he had caught a whiff of the many gourmet meals we had set out for the animals to enjoy. He stood on top of the squirrel feeder, which was full of the best squirrel food you can buy, and held his nose high, desperately trying to track the scent of his next meal. I smiled, knowing he was about to enjoy the jackpot beneath his feet.

To my surprise, instead of using the squirrel feeder to enjoy a feast, he simply used it as a step stool to climb off the fence and down into the yard. He cautiously made his way under one of the bird feeders that hung in the tree above. I watched as he spent the next ten minutes scrounging through the leftover birdseed the birds had tossed away. He had no idea a delicious meal had already been set out for him just feet away.

> **Sometimes I wonder if God watches us scrounge through dirty leftovers when he has prepared a feast for us to enjoy.**

Sometimes I wonder if God watches us scrounge through dirty leftovers when he has prepared a feast for us to enjoy.

God has invited us to join him on the greatest adventure the world has ever known. He is redeeming our shattered hearts, community, and world. And for some reason, he chooses us to be part of that rescue mission.

Try wrapping your head around the God of the entire universe enlisting you to bring chunks of heaven down here to earth. When you do, it's hard to imagine being bored.

The truth is, though, that we step right over that invitation and make our way down to the yard to pick through the scraps. We settle for crumbs like porn, alcohol, or new toys, knowing full well they won't satisfy. Our appetite for adventure leads us back to our sin over and over again. Or as the writer of Proverbs says, "Like a dog that returns to his vomit is a fool who repeats his folly" (Proverbs 26:11).

As I sat and watched that squirrel rummage through the leftover birdseed, I felt a little sorry for him. He had no idea what he was missing out on. He was trying to satisfy his appetite with crumbs when I had worked hard to prepare him a feast.

> **Christ gave up his life to call us friends and invite us to work with him, yet we choose to find adventure elsewhere.**

How much more did the Father sacrifice for us to enjoy a feast with him? We were enemies of God, but because of what Christ did on the cross, we are now friends of God. That's crazy. Christ gave up his life to call us friends and invite us to work with him, yet we choose to find adventure elsewhere.

I know it seems a bit weird to compare our lives with God to a squirrel finding food in my backyard, but I can't help but wonder how much God's heart must break to see us scrounging through leftovers to fulfill our appetites when he knows a feast is just feet away.

ROCKS AND TREES AND YOU AND ME

It's hard to imagine the men of the Bible being bored. I'm sure they had plenty of mundane days, but the overall story of their lives must have been anything but boring.

Abraham was called to pick up his family and move to an unknown land. Later he was told he would have a son when he was a hundred years old—and that son would bless the nations.

God invited Moses to help rescue his people out of slavery in Egypt. Moses watched the seas part, food miraculously appear from heaven, and God show up through a burning bush.

Jesus invited Peter to leave his job and join him in his ministry. Later, Jesus invited him to walk on water with him in the middle of a storm as part of an impromptu faith lesson.

God literally knocked Paul to the ground and invited him to turn from his evil ways. God later used Paul to plant churches around the region and become a major catalyst in the advancement of the early church.

Rest assured, these men were not bored. God used them to play a small role in the redemption of the world, and their lives revolved around that mission.

Several years ago, I discipled a group of boys during their senior year of high school. These boys were studs—athletic, smart, and well-liked by their peers. Every week they came to my house, and we talked about following Jesus in their everyday lives.

I didn't envy these guys. They faced an insane amount of temptation every day. We all deal with temptation, but it seems the enemy has his own temptation lab experiment on high school campuses around the country. These young men were being hit from every possible direction.

At the end of the year, before they headed off to college, I told them I would take them anywhere in the world they wanted to go. We had spent the entire year together, and I wanted to end it with a memorable experience.

Instead of picking a typical "senior trip" on a tropical island, the boys decided they wanted to serve together. The devastating earthquake in Haiti had occurred earlier that year, and the guys decided they wanted to use their senior trip to serve and encourage the Haitian people. I had never been to Haiti before, but I was committed to finding a way to make this trip happen with them.

We spent the next several months raising funds and planning our trip out of the country. By God's grace, we gathered all the prayer and financial support needed and made our way to Haiti.

I've traveled to dozens of countries around the world, but none like Haiti. It is a beautiful country, but it's completely devastated by natural disasters and a severely broken economy. As we drove through the streets, our hearts broke with a sense of hopelessness for the people. Witchcraft is extremely popular among the locals, and a heaviness lingered in our souls as we heard about the brokenness and evil around us.

This is not how things were supposed to be, I thought repeatedly during the trip.

> Amid all the rubble and brokenness, there were small glimmers of hope and redemption.

And yet amid all the rubble and brokenness, there were small glimmers of hope and redemption. God had not given up on the country of Haiti, and he had not forgotten its people. In this very moment, he is taking what is broken and making it new. And in our short eight-day trip to that little island, we got to join in with him to play a tiny role in that redemptive work. We worked with the locals to build houses, clean streets, pray for people who were hurting, and encourage our brothers and sisters in Christ. God used us in a very small way to bring chunks of heaven here to earth.

At the end of the week, as we gathered to have one final talk before heading home, one thing struck me. Normally, when we'd get together at my house each week, the guys would talk about how hard it was to fight temptation and live righteously. But this week was different. I saw a side of the guys that I hadn't seen all year. They weren't thinking about temptations and struggles as they normally would. Instead, they were excited to wake up each morning to see how God might use them for the day. They had the eyes and mindset of missionaries. They prayed together constantly. They saw every interaction as an opportunity to show the love of Christ. They sacrificed for each other and the people they came to serve. Every moment felt exciting as they thought about what God could do next or what he was about to show them.

I wonder if this is how the guys we read about in the Scriptures felt. Of course, they continued to deal with sin and temptation, but I wonder if they also woke up every morning eager to see how God would move around them. I imagine we'd be more likely to avoid the sins that so easily entangle us (see Hebrews 12:1) if we focused on the way God was using us in his redemptive story rather than focusing on avoiding temptation. I wonder if the arguments we have with our wives and kids would diminish if we remembered we were partnering with God in his work to bring a little piece of heaven here to earth.

> **We'd be more likely to avoid the sins that so easily entangle us if we focused on the way God was using us in his redemptive story rather than focusing on avoiding temptation.**

During that week in Haiti, we were still the same old group of broken and messed-up young dudes we were the week before. Nothing significant had changed—except that we realized we didn't have to let our sin stop us from being used by God. We finally believed the Holy Spirit could work in us, and despite of us, to bring parts of his kingdom to Haiti. We were excited and found great adventure in partnering with God in his work. And because of that, we seemed to focus less on our little worlds and our personal sins and more on the bigger story that was happening around us.

Sometimes I get so caught up in the day-to-day grind of life that I forget the amazing work God has been doing since that famous day back in the garden. From the very first pages of Scripture, God has been working to turn things back to the way they were supposed to be. He knows what the world was like when it wasn't broken, when our hearts weren't broken, when our relationships with him and each other weren't broken...and he won't stop until all things are made new again (see Revelation 21:4).

> **God could fix this whole world by himself. He could use the rocks and the trees to redeem mankind. For some reason, though, he invites us to tag along.**

The crazy part to me, though, is that he doesn't just do that work by himself. He invites us to tag along.

Sometimes when I'm fixing something around the house, I'll invite Elijah to help me out. I don't invite him to help me because he is a master carpenter or because he has freakish handyman skills for a seven-year-old. In fact, he's quite the opposite. He still doesn't know how to properly use a hammer, and I have to keep reminding him which way to turn the screwdriver. One time he almost chopped off my hand with a chop saw.

I could do things faster and better if I did the work on my own. But I wouldn't trade our partnership for the world. I want nothing more than for him to work alongside me.

I'm confident God could fix this whole world by himself. He could use the rocks and the trees to redeem mankind. For some reason, though, he invites us to tag along, even if it means we might accidentally chop his hand off (or like Peter, chop someone's ear off). We tend to get in the way and make a mess of things. But God doesn't kick us off to the side—he continues to let us join him in his adventurous rescue project.

Partnering with God to see lives changed is way more thrilling than fantasy football, a new Jet Ski, or getting drunk with your friends. He wants you to join him in a much more exciting adventure.

Don't get distracted by the leftovers on the lawn when God has prepared a feast just a few feet away.

TAILGATE PRAYERS

What if you were like the guys of the Bible or the high school guys I took to Haiti? What if you saw yourself as a missionary? How would life change for you with this perspective?

There was a time in our marriage when Leila and I worked especially hard to live like missionaries in our neighborhood. I kept thinking, *If we really do serve the God of creation, who is always actively pursuing the world, then we should be constantly seeing him work around us.* I figured that if I wasn't seeing God working, the problem was not that God was idle but that I simply wasn't seeing what he was doing. So we committed to living our lives as missionaries and looking for ways to see God in every situation.

During this season, we happened to be moving from our little apartment into a new house. I got lazy and was looking for every possible way to not have to carry the heavy furniture down three flights of stairs. One item in particular, our bed frame, had been haunting me all week. It was a beast, made of solid wood, and weighed more than

> **Partnering with God to see lives changed is way more thrilling than fantasy football, a new Jet Ski, or getting drunk with your friends. He wants you to join him in a much more exciting adventure.**

I could imagine. I seriously considered setting it on fire so I wouldn't have to carry it down the stairs.

Instead, I convinced Leila that we needed a new bed frame and that this was the perfect time to sell our old one. (Let someone else lug it out of our apartment!) The Spirit must have been working in her heart, because she agreed that now would be a great time to get rid of the bed frame. Without hesitating, I immediately pulled out my phone, snapped some photos, listed it on Craigslist, and began disassembling it.

The next day I got a call from a guy saying he'd like to come pick up the frame. In my mind, it was a win-win. He'd carry it down the stairs, and I'd make a little extra cash. To my great disappointment, he showed up alone and needed help loading the bed frame into his truck. As we stood in my nearly empty bedroom, I took a few minutes to show him how to reassemble the frame.

As I talked about the nuts and bolts, I felt God speak to my Spirit. I rarely make statements like that because I feel that such language is often overused and abused in the church. But I knew for sure that this thought was not my own. I had been praying with Leila all week about us living as missionaries and looking for ways to see God move around us, and I was confident he was answering our prayers at that moment.

Give him the bed frame. That thought went through my mind over and over.

I don't want to give him the bed frame. I want the cash so I can buy a new bed frame for Leila and me, I argued in my head.

Give him the bed frame for free.

I was having what felt like a bipolar meltdown in the middle of my Craigslist transaction.

Finally, I relented.

"Hey, man, I'd like to just give you this bed frame," I said out loud as my heart nearly pounded out of my chest.

"What?" the guy said.

"Yeah, dude, I just feel like I need to give you this bed frame. I think we've been blessed so we can be a blessing."

I could tell that last sentence totally confused him.

"Are you serious?" he responded.

"Yep. It'd be a joy for me to give this to you. I'll help you load it up."

I couldn't believe what I was saying. This was the worst-case scenario. Not only was I not going to make any extra cash, but now I was about to do exactly what I was trying to avoid—carry the stupid bed frame down three flights of stairs.

All my plans were being ruined. But apparently I wasn't the only one with a plan that night.

As we picked up the bed frame and made our way down the stairs, the man stopped and looked at me.

"My wife just served me with divorce papers and kicked me out of the house. I needed a new bed frame because I don't have any furniture or a place to sleep. I can't tell you how much it means to me that you're just giving it to me like this."

My heart sank, and I fought back tears.

"Bro, I am so sorry. I can't imagine what you're going through right now."

"Yeah, man…I have three little girls too. I'm a wreck. I don't know what I'm going to do."

We made our way to the bottom of the stairs and loaded the frame into his truck. God had clearly invited me into something big here, and I didn't want to miss out on what he was doing.

"Hey, man, I know this seems a little weird, but would it be cool if I prayed with you?"

"That would seriously mean the world to me," he responded.

We sat on the tailgate of his truck as I pleaded to God to restore their marriage. I asked God to protect his heart from bitterness and his little girls' hearts from overwhelming pain. We finished praying, hopped off the back of the truck, and gave each other a hug after exchanging phone numbers.

> **Maybe taking up my cross had less to do with me dying physically and more to do with me dying to my comforts. Maybe it meant me dying to the lies I was believing about what would satisfy my soul.**

As he drove away that night, I couldn't help but think about the opportunity I would have missed had I not listened to God's prompting of my heart. The truth is, God was already pursuing that guy, and he could have used anyone to join in. But by his grace, he invited me into that moment. The work was going to get done no matter what, but I got the chance to see it with my own eyes.

The experience lit a fire in me. I couldn't fall asleep that night. I kept thinking about all the little pieces that had to come together for that moment to happen. It amazed me to think that God had been orchestrating all the details while I simply thought I was trying to avoid moving a bed frame down a few flights of stairs.

I went to bed excited, eager to wake up the next day to see what God would invite me into next.

The next several weeks were amazing. As I woke up every day with the mindset of a missionary, I looked for ways God could use me to bring his kingdom to earth. I had more intentional conversations about Jesus than I'd had in years. I made new friends, saw broken relationships restored, fell more in love with my wife, and felt more excitement as a follower of Jesus than I had ever felt.

But do you know what happened next? Eventually I started to believe the lie that adventure can be found elsewhere. I became convinced there were more exciting things to chase after than life on a mission with Jesus. In many ways, I got comfortable. It takes a lot of faith to live as a missionary. You have to step into conversations you wouldn't normally step into. You talk with more strangers. And sometimes God even asks you to give stuff away.

Eventually, I stopped wanting to have those conversations with random people at the grocery store. I didn't want to step into potentially hard or awkward conversations anymore. And I became convinced it was better to keep my stuff than to give it away.

Maybe this is what Jesus meant in Mark 8:34: "If anyone would come after me, let him deny himself and take up his cross and follow me."

Maybe taking up my cross had less to do with me dying physically and more to do with me dying to my comforts. Maybe it meant me dying to the lies I was believing about what would satisfy my soul.

> **I don't want our families to miss out on the best with Jesus because we're chasing after comfort and safety. I don't want my kids to see their dad pursuing adventure in things that have no eternal value.**

TERRIBLE GODS

Even as I sit in my living room and write this chapter, I am conflicted. I'm writing this book on an expensive laptop that I purchased in hopes that it would bring me more joy. On my left hand is an Apple Watch that I was convinced would bring me happiness. I'm pausing to look up around my living room and see all the things I have spent my money on, desperately hoping to find some contentment.

I can tell you now that those things suck at being God.

Nothing in this home has satisfied my soul like Jesus can. Nothing is quite as exhilarating and rewarding as stepping out in faith with the God of the universe and going to work for the sake of his kingdom.

Why do we chase such dumb and trivial things? I want to get back to the place where I am waking up every morning excited to see God work and courageous enough to step out in faith when he invites me in.

BACK TO THE TABLE

My original plan to end this chapter was to challenge you to see yourself more like a missionary. But I think I would be purposely avoiding what the Spirit is trying to do inside me if I didn't lump myself into that challenge.

Brother, will you join me in ditching the leftover birdseed on the ground and sitting at the table with the King?

> **Your soul doesn't want more football, more porn, more money, or more toys. Your soul wants Jesus.**

Maybe that squirrel in my backyard felt safer rummaging through leftover birdseed on the ground. Maybe it was too dangerous or he felt too vulnerable to enjoy the feast I had left for him by the fence. But in his hunt for safety and comfort, he missed out on the best.

I don't want our families to miss out on the best with Jesus because we're chasing after comfort and safety. I don't want my kids to see their dad pursuing adventure in things that have no eternal value.

What if instead of playing it safe, you saw your family as a mission team sent by God into the neighborhood where you live? God has given your family unique qualities and characteristics. You can choose to hoard them for yourself, or you can step out in faith and be salt and light where God has placed you. In doing so, you will likely fall into conversations with your neighbors when it would be easier to shut the garage door. It might require you to spend more money on food so you can feed a widow or a struggling student. It might mean buying an extra bike so the neighborhood kids can play at your house.

Believe me, living as a missionary isn't easy. It requires a lot of sacrifice when it comes to your time, your money, and your comfort. It would be much easier to take the more comfortable route. But I can assure you, the comfortable route will not satisfy the longing for adventure that God has placed deep within your soul.

> **Ditch the worldly adventures you've been chasing after and lead your family toward the adventures of God.**

Your soul doesn't want more football, more porn, more money, or more toys. Your soul wants Jesus. You are hardwired, deep within your very being, to search for what is right. Your spirit recognizes when something isn't the way it's supposed to be, and it won't be settled until it is.

Get off the ground and come to the table. There is a feast here. Find the adventure your soul is longing for by working with God as he restores your broken neighborhood. Foster or adopt a child. Invite a coworker's family over for dinner. Have the neighborhood kids over for a movie night. Take your family to serve in a local charity—or in an orphanage halfway around the world. Move. Give up your stuff. Give up your time and comfort. God is moving all around you, and he is already at work. Ditch the worldly adventures you've been chasing after and lead your family toward the adventures of God.

PART 3

THE KINGDOM OF GOD THROUGH YOU

7

LOST IN THE WOODS

Why All of Life Is Family Devotional Time

When I was in high school, I came across a show called *Man vs. Wild* hosted by a guy named Bear Grylls. Bear was an absolute stud. A film crew followed him as he survived some of the most dangerous and remote locations in the world. He jumped out of planes, ate dead carcasses, and built fires without matches. Regardless of the situation, Bear figured out a way to survive.

I fell so in love with the show, and specifically with Bear Grylls, that I ended up buying his survival book and learning everything I could about surviving the harshest conditions in the world. I remember staying up late at night and skipping my homework so I could learn new survival techniques. I figured if a zombie apocalypse happened, I would need the skills I learned from Bear Grylls, not the ones I learned from my twelfth-grade math teacher.

After months of binge-watching the show and countless nights studying the book, I decided it was time to put my own skills to the test. I was confident in my newfound ability to survive whatever dangers the world decided to throw my way. Despite my mom's deep concern for my safety, I loaded up my backpack with a couple of protein bars and drove several hours to the closest wilderness area I could find.

I arrived at a trailhead at the base of the Sierra Mountains and hopped out of the car, almost laughing at the thought that this forest would try to stop a guy like me from surviving. I had never gone backpacking before, but I had studied hard and was confident I could channel my inner Bear Grylls.

I spent the next few hours hiking deep into the woods. Finding a source of water was my top priority, and then I would set up shelter. Without a map and with no real sense of direction, I wandered aimlessly, hoping the right spot would miraculously appear to me. Two hours turned into four and four into six. Daylight faded to dusk, and soon it was pitch black.

I lay down in the middle of the forest, using my nearly empty backpack as a pillow, and quietly started to panic. I was terrified. I had no food, no water, no shelter, and absolutely no idea what I was going to do.

Then I heard something. It was probably a family of squirrels, but in the moment, I was sure a pack of wolves had surrounded me.

Despite what I had taught myself about wilderness survival, I rejected sound judgment and decided to try to return to the car, using my cell phone as a flashlight. I had no intention of being eaten alive out there, and I was determined to get home as quickly as possible.

To this day, I have no idea how I found my way back to the parking lot in the middle of the night. But by God's grace, I jumped into my car and made my way home as quickly as possible.

Halfway through my drive home, I pulled over at a McDonald's to grab a late dinner. Sitting in that empty restaurant and eating a twenty-piece Chicken McNuggets meal, I wondered what had gone wrong. I had studied Bear Grylls's book for hours. I had watched dozens of *Man vs. Wild* episodes. And yet I couldn't even survive ten hours on my own in the wild.

As it turns out, watching TV and reading books don't adequately prepare someone to experience the real thing.

But I still hadn't learned that lesson.

I later watched a documentary about CrossFit athletes on Netflix.[1] I had heard about CrossFit but didn't know what all the hype was about. The documentary followed athletes as they trained for and participated in the most grueling of physical competitions. These were some of the fittest human beings on earth.

So I, still naive and no smarter after my failed Bear Grylls experience, decided I could probably do what I saw these athletes doing on TV.

No kidding—the next morning, I woke Leila and the kids and told them we were joining a gym. Leila gave me a weird look and said, "Are you sure about this, babe? You get winded after slicing an apple for the kids."

"Absolutely. I watched a documentary last night, and I'm feeling motivated."

Before long, we had packed up the car and were headed to the local YMCA. As Leila was filling out the paperwork for us to join, I was looking through their list of classes. I noticed they had a muscle conditioning class, which sounded most like the CrossFit routine I had watched the night before.

Most of us want our kids to love Jesus but don't really know where to begin.

"Are we able to start attending classes right away?" I asked the lady behind the desk.

"Definitely. You can start now if you'd like," she replied.

I didn't have my exercise clothes on, but I figured I could make it work. The class started in ten minutes, so I told Leila to explore the new gym with the kids while I went downstairs to work out.

---

[1] Yes, you are sensing a theme here. I need to stop watching shows.

To my surprise, when I arrived at the class, I was the only male in attendance.

"Is this a coed class?" I asked the instructor.

"Yes, of course!" she replied, smiling and welcoming me in.

> **If we're not careful, family devotional time can become just another item to check off our parenting to-do list.**

I gathered all the necessary equipment and headed to the back of the room. While stretching, I began to look around at my classmates. I was not only the lone dude in the class but also the only one under the age of fifty. These women looked as if they were on a field trip from the assisted-living center down the road. I started to doubt whether I was going to get a workout like the one I had seen on TV.

"All right, ladies, let's get started with warm-ups!" the instructor shouted.

We were about twenty-two minutes into the workout when I realized what a terrible decision I had made. I could feel the Captain Crunch I had eaten an hour earlier starting to slosh around in my stomach. I gave it five more jumping jacks before I ran over to the nearest trash can and started to lose it.

One of the sweet old ladies came over and rubbed my back. "Are you okay, hon?" she asked. She didn't have a drop of sweat on her.

"Yes, of course—I think I just ate something weird," I said as I grabbed my belongings and tried to sneak out.

Once again I had been taught a valuable lesson. Watching CrossFit documentaries and reading about the routine didn't make me fit.

WAFFLE HEADS

At least once a week, someone from the Dad Tired community reaches out to me and asks me to recommend a family devotional. It's not surprising, since most of us want our kids to love Jesus but don't really know where to begin. Family devotionals can seem like an easy place to start.

When I'm asked this question, I always mention the Dad Tired resources page,[2] but I follow up by asking, "What are you really wanting to accomplish with your kids?"

I think the question catches most people off guard because it's kind of direct and in-your-face. Most people respond with something like "I just want to teach my kids the Bible" or "I want my kids to love God, but I'm not really sure how to teach them to do that."

We parents are constantly looking for the best resources to help us raise our children. I'm always on the hunt for the latest food trends, school resources, educational music, and brain-stimulating activities.

If we're not careful, though, family devotional time can become just another item to check off our parenting to-do list.

I know that sounds harsh, so let me explain.

When I was on church pastoral staffs, I watched parents do everything in their power to raise smart and successful children. They put their kids in the best schools, signed them up for the best sports teams, enrolled them in music lessons or other extracurricular activities, and then dropped them off at church to give them a good dose of "Jesus time."

> **Their families had nailed the devotional time but somehow missed the goal of making disciples.**

I couldn't help but notice that everything seemed to fit nicely into little compartments.

---

[2] See www.dadtired.com/resources.

There was a time for school. A time for sports. A time for homework. A time for lessons. And then a time for Jesus.

In fact, some of the best parents at our church were amazingly disciplined at having "Jesus time" at home every night before bed.

> **I don't want my kids to be experts in Bible stories and yet be far from God.**

The problem was that while many of these kids could recite every Bible story from memory, their hearts were still far from God. Their families had nailed the devotional time but somehow missed the goal of making disciples. These kids would sit in my office and share about their lives, revealing that they actually had no clue what it meant to follow Jesus in real life.

We Americans love compartments. We keep everything separated and in its proper place. This is especially true for men. In their book *Men Are Like Waffles—Women Are Like Spaghetti*, Bill and Pam Farrel describe the way men compartmentalize each segment of life into little squares, like a waffle. Women, on the other hand, tend to see everything as being interconnected, like spaghetti.

If we're not careful, we can become dads who raise our kids to see Jesus as only one part of their lives, one square of the waffle. If we're not intentional, our children will begin to learn that Daddy has a time to coach baseball, a time to help with homework, a time to be at work, and a time to talk about God before bed. They will soon realize that following Jesus isn't an all-consuming thing but rather a compartmentalized kind of thing.

I don't want my kids to be experts in Bible stories and yet be far from God. In fact, I don't know if there is anything worse. I'm confident you don't want that either. You don't want to just check off the "Jesus" box on your parenting to-do list.

So I'll ask you the same question I constantly ask the men of our Dad Tired community: What do you really want to accomplish with your kids?

Do you want your kids to be passionate followers of Jesus or simply moral people? Do you long to see them follow in the footsteps of Christ or merely gain some spiritual values?

I'm confident you are not willing to settle for simply raising moral kids. I'm guessing you're all-in when it comes to raising children who will love God with all their heart, soul, mind, and strength.

So let's learn from the King himself how to help broken and messy people fall in love with him.

IN EVERY SITUATION

When it comes to learning how to raise children who love God, one of my favorite passages of Scripture is in Deuteronomy 6. Listen to what Moses says:

> You shall love the LORD your God with all your heart and with all your soul and with all your might. And these words that I command you today shall be on your heart. You shall teach them diligently to your children, and shall talk of them when you sit in your house, and when you walk by the way, and when you lie down, and when you rise. You shall bind them as a sign on your hand, and they shall be as frontlets between your eyes. You shall write them on the doorposts of your house and on your gates (verses 5-9).

I love the way Moses instructs people to teach their children, emphasizing that we must first be in love with God with all our heart, soul, and might. It's hard to give your children what you don't personally possess. For Moses, raising kids who love God clearly goes way deeper than checking off a box; it requires an all-consuming devotion to loving him.

And then, as we are falling in love with God and his words, we are instructed to teach these things to our kids. But catch this—Moses didn't say to teach them for fifteen minutes before we go to bed. Instead, he says, "You shall teach them diligently to your children, and shall talk of them when you sit in your house, and when you walk by the way, and when you lie down, and when you rise."

> **For Moses and the people of the Old Testament, every moment was an opportunity to point their kids back to God.**

What Moses is describing here is the opposite of compartmentalization. There is no such thing as "God time." Instead, we are to talk to our children about God when we sit, and when we walk, and when we lie down, and when we wake up. For Moses and the people of the Old Testament, every moment was an opportunity to point their kids back to God.

I imagine that if Moses had written this passage in AD 2019 instead of 1220(ish) BC, it would have read something like this:

> Brothers, fall in love with God with every ounce of your being. Study his Word and keep it close to your heart. Teach it to your kids every opportunity you get—when you're getting groceries, when you're throwing a baseball in the backyard, when you're eating dinner at a restaurant, and when you're hanging out at a barbecue with your neighbors. Keep your eyes open for any opportunity to point your children back to their Creator.

I'm sure it would have been a little more eloquent and Moses-like, but you get the idea.

Raising kids who are passionately in love with Jesus seems to involve two things: a dad who is himself passionately in love with Jesus and one who is willing to teach his kids about him in every situation.

According to Moses, we are called to much more than a simple devotional time every night or a couple of times a week. God desires a heart completely in love with him and a dedication to teach our children at every waking hour.

When Jesus shows up on the scene hundreds of years later, he models for us what Moses was talking about.

Have you ever wondered what the Bible would be like if Jesus trained his twelve disciples the same way we train people in our churches? Imagine Jesus walking into the Jewish temple and listening to a reading of the Scriptures. At the end of the service, he starts chatting it up with some other guys. They seem to hit it off, so Jesus says, "Hey, man, we should get together on Tuesday mornings and study the Scriptures over some coffee."

> **For Jesus, it wasn't enough for his disciples to simply know the Scriptures; he wanted them to practice what they meant by living them out in real life.**

"Uh, yeah…that sounds cool," Peter says reluctantly.

And then the rest of the Gospels are filled with stories of them meeting once a week at Starbucks and talking about what they learned. Half the time Peter is late because he sleeps in, or he cancels because his schedule is a little too busy.

Thankfully for us, Jesus didn't take our modern-day approach to discipleship. Instead, he followed the example Moses set in Deuteronomy. He invited Peter to give up his job as a fisherman and join him on an adventure rescuing the world by fishing for men. Peter and the rest of the disciples had no idea what it meant to fish for men, but they soon learned—not from once-a-week Bible studies but from seeing the Scriptures come alive as Jesus walked, and talked, and sat, and lay down, and ate. Just as Moses wrote in

Raising kids
who are passionately
in love with Jesus
seems to involve two things:
a dad who is himself passionately
in love with Jesus
and one who is willing
to teach his kids about him
in every situation.

Deuteronomy, Jesus used every possible opportunity to make disciples who loved the Lord their God with all their heart, soul, and might.

Jesus didn't throw out the Scriptures; he paired them with real-life situations so the disciples could truly know what they meant. He taught them that to be disciples, they had to humble themselves and serve. Then he showed them how in real life by getting on his knees to wash their dirty feet or having them serve the hungry crowds who were without food. He taught them what the Scriptures said about the Sabbath and then took advantage of situations that put their views of the Sabbath to the test. For Jesus, it wasn't enough for his disciples to simply know the Scriptures. He wanted them to practice what they meant by living them out in real life.

THE NARROW PATH

Last week I was reading a story to my kids from the book of Matthew. When we got to Matthew 7, Elijah had me reread this verse:

> Enter through the narrow gate. For wide is the gate and broad is the road that leads to destruction, and many enter through it. But small is the gate and narrow the road that leads to life, and only a few find it (Matthew 7:13-14 NIV).

"What does that mean, Daddy?" he asked.

I tried to explain that Jesus was teaching his disciples that many people will choose not to follow him. We talked about how even though following our own ways often leads to destruction, most people will still take that road. The road Jesus calls us to is narrower and therefore harder, and very few people will actually find it and choose to follow it.

"How is following Jesus hard? That doesn't make any sense. Who wouldn't want to follow Jesus?" he asked, clearly confused by the passage and my explanation.

I laughed. "I know, son. It seems crazy now. But you will learn that following Jesus isn't easy. In fact, it's a lot easier not to follow him."

"That doesn't make any sense," he said as I kissed his forehead and tucked him into bed.

Two days later we went to the gym, and I dropped him off in the child-care play area while I went to my workout class.[3] After the class, when I picked him up, the teacher pulled me aside and asked if she could talk to me in private. I have never had any problems with Elijah, so I was caught off guard. She explained to me that Elijah had been disrespectful during class and had to be told multiple times to stop misbehaving. I was embarrassed and had him apologize to her for his behavior.

> Following Jesus isn't easy. In fact, it's a lot easier not to follow him.

By the time we got to the car, I was livid. I gave him a stern speech and told him he was grounded from his bike and friends for the next few days. He was abnormally quiet in the back seat. I turned around to look at him and saw that he was quietly crying while looking out the window.

"Dude, what's going on?" I asked.

He didn't answer but continued crying. By this time, my anger had subsided, and my heart was starting to soften up.

"What's going on, buddy? You can talk to me."

Fighting through the tears, he began telling me about two older girls in the class who were making fun of him in front of everyone. He had asked them to stop, but they'd only persisted.

---

[3] Yep, that class. Shut your mouth.

"I was so mad, Daddy. I wanted to make them feel worse than they were making me feel."

I nodded. "I get it, son. I've felt that way too. You wanna know something crazy that Jesus said?"

"Sure."

I opened my Bible app to the book of Luke and turned on the audio through the car speakers.

> I say to you who hear, Love your enemies, do good to those who hate you, bless those who curse you, pray for those who abuse you. To one who strikes you on the cheek, offer the other also, and from one who takes away your cloak do not withhold your tunic either. Give to everyone who begs from you, and from one who takes away your goods do not demand them back. And as you wish that others would do to you, do so to them.
>
> If you love those who love you, what benefit is that to you? For even sinners love those who love them. And if you do good to those who do good to you, what benefit is that to you? For even sinners do the same. And if you lend to those from whom you expect to receive, what credit is that to you? Even sinners lend to sinners, to get back the same amount. But love your enemies, and do good, and lend, expecting nothing in return, and your reward will be great, and you will be sons of the Most High, for he is kind to the ungrateful and the evil. Be merciful, even as your Father is merciful (Luke 6:27-36).

He sat quietly and listened almost as if he were in shock. When the verse had ended, he said, "What? Why would anyone ever love their enemies? I could never love those girls."

"I know it's hard, son. Most people will choose to take the wide, easy road and treat their enemies the way they've been treated. Following Jesus's way is hard. Very few people will want to do it."

We sat silently in the parking lot as the Spirit of God allowed those words to sink in. I could tell that he remembered the words he had said just a few nights earlier and that this lesson was moving off the pages of Scripture and deep into the depths of his little heart.

"I want you to go home tonight and think about whether you really want to follow Jesus. I know how hard it is, son…trust me. It would be much easier to take the wide road. Give it some thought."

The next morning we woke up and were sitting around the table eating breakfast together as a family. I asked Elijah if he had thought about our conversation from the day before. He nodded his head.

"What did you decide?" I asked.

"I want to find the narrow path," he said quietly.

My eyes welled up with tears.

> **God has always paired the truth of his Word with the realities of this life to teach us what it means to follow him.**

The God who used the Scriptures and real-life circumstances to teach his disciples how to follow him is the same God who used Scripture and a real-life circumstance to draw my son's heart to him.

Elijah didn't repeat a fancy prayer. He didn't say he wanted to follow Jesus because he wants to go to heaven one day. Instead, he began to learn, from both the Scriptures and real life, what it means to count the cost, die to self, and follow Jesus.

Here's the thing: It's easy to watch a bunch of Netflix documentaries and think you're an expert at something. It's easy to pick up a book from Amazon and convince yourself you can go survive out in the woods. But it's a completely different thing to actually experience it. To live it. To let life teach you the principles you thought you already knew.

Moses knew the beautiful combination of loving God's words and applying them to real-life situations. Jesus loved his disciples enough to teach them the Word of God and then put them in situations where they would have to apply it.

Our little Elijah felt confident he could follow Jesus after reading his words in our family devotional. But he learned a new lesson when he found himself in a difficult situation and was asked to live out from his heart what he thought he already knew in his head.

If my family didn't study the Word, our son would have never known that Jesus asked him to do what feels impossible to do alone. And if the Holy Spirit hadn't used a real-life situation to apply those teachings, they would have been stuck in his head and never made their way down into the depths of his heart.

God has always paired the truth of his Word with the realities of this life to teach us what it means to follow him.

RIVERS AND PHONES

Think back on your own life and the times you learned some of the most valuable life lessons. Most likely they were learned not just through a Bible study but through seeing God's Word applied in real life.

Last summer my mom and sister flew up from California to visit our family here in Oregon. I like to take the kids fishing at a river near our house, so I invited them to tag along for the day. We set up some chairs and a picnic on the dock and spent the day fishing for bass. We had been there for several hours without much action when suddenly my sister's rod bent almost all the way into the water. I jumped out of my chair and helped her reel in the biggest bass we had ever seen at that dock. She hadn't been fishing since she was a young girl, so she asked me to pull out my phone and take some pictures. Otherwise her husband wouldn't have believed she'd caught such a big fish!

I took the photo and tried to put my phone back into my pocket, but it slipped out of my hands and sank to the bottom of the river.

All of us gasped simultaneously, almost as if we had just watched a car accident happen in front of us.

"Well, that sucks," I said as I started laughing.

"Yeah, and now no one will believe the size of the fish I just caught and threw back!" my sister said while slapping my shoulder.

We all laughed, packed up our stuff, and headed home.

> **I surprised myself with my own anger.**

Leila and I are in the middle of trying to become debt-free, so instead of making payments on a new phone, we just used some of our savings to pay cash.

The next week, we went back to that same dock to do some more fishing. My mom and sister had returned to California, so this time it was just me and the kids. After a couple of slow hours, my four-year-old daughter asked if she could watch cartoons on my new phone. I told her absolutely not because I was worried about dropping my phone in the river again.

"I promise I will be careful, Daddy."

I gave in and handed her my new phone.[4] I made her sit in the middle of the dock so that if she accidentally dropped the phone, it couldn't possibly end up in the water.

A few minutes passed, and then she said, "Daddy, the internet isn't working."

"Give it a minute…it will come back."

---

[4] You think you know where this is going, but you don't.

She waited about thirteen more seconds until her four-year-old body and brain made the decision that she had used up her supply of patience for the day. With a shout of frustration, she threw the phone as far as she could into the river.

I watched, almost as if in slow motion, as my four-day-old phone made its way into the air, hit the water, and sank to the bottom.

Two phones at the bottom of the river in five days. Fully paid for. No insurance.

To say I screamed at the top of my lungs would be an understatement. In fact, I have never heard myself scream like that. I even surprised myself with my own anger. My son, with his incredibly high emotional intelligence, assessed the situation immediately and began packing up our stuff. My daughter started crying, perhaps because of my yelling or perhaps because *Peppa Pig* hadn't loaded quickly enough.

Back at the parking lot, I threw everything in the trunk and slammed the car doors. My blood was boiling. I'm embarrassed to say I screamed at my four-year-old daughter the entire car ride home. It was the worst parenting moment of my life.

> I screamed at my four-year-old daughter the entire car ride home. It was the worst parenting moment of my life.

That night I went to bed angry because of the money I had lost. Angry with my daughter's behavior. Angry that I was failing as a parent and didn't know how to raise well-behaved kids. Angry at myself for responding poorly to the situation and yelling at our little girl. I was angry at everything.

I woke up the next morning phoneless and unable to distract myself. I was forced to sit in the quietness of my own thoughts, which I think God used to his advantage. As I reflected on the events of the day before, my anger began to settle and turn into feelings of guilt and shame. In the quiet, I felt the whispers of the Holy Spirit speaking to my undistracted soul.

> *If I can take care of the birds of the air, I can take care of you.*
>
> *I love your daughter more than you do. It's okay if you feel out of control with her. I am not out of control.*
>
> *My grace is sufficient for your anger. Repent. Ask your daughter for forgiveness. Move on.*

The same Jesus who used Scripture and real-life circumstances to teach his disciples how to be more like him was using Scripture and a real-life circumstance to draw my heart back to him.

I wish that by simply reading the Scriptures, I could have learned a lesson about my anger or my desire to be in control. But for me, it took both the Scriptures and the tough reality of life to make my heart more like his.

> **Your children need more than a daddy who will read the latest devotional to them a couple of times a week. They need a daddy who is committed to helping them apply those scriptural truths in everyday life.**

EVERYTHING IS A DEVOTIONAL

If we are serious about raising passionate disciples of God, we must throw away our compartmentalized thinking and begin following the way of Jesus. Your children need more than a daddy who will read the latest devotional to them a couple of times a week. They need a daddy who is committed to helping them apply those scriptural truths in everyday life. They need to be taught the Word as they are sitting and walking and eating and playing.

Raising children who fall in love with Jesus involves a lot of studying God's Word together, but it also involves a bunch of thirty-second reminders of how their current circumstances allow them to live out what they are learning in God's Word.

When my children comment about someone's looks at the grocery store, I remind them that God made everyone in his image.

When my kids are struck by the colors of the sunset, I remind them of God's creativity.

When my kids enjoy a good meal at our home or a restaurant, I remind them that God is a good provider who faithfully meets our needs.

When my kids have a hard time sharing their toys with friends, I remind them that God shared his best things, including himself, with us.

Spiritual leaders don't just do family devotionals. They see all of life as a family devotional and use every opportunity to point their kids toward Jesus.

> **Spiritual leaders don't just do family devotionals. They see all of life as a family devotional and use every opportunity to point their kids toward Jesus.**

At the end of his earthly ministry, Jesus told his disciples to go into all the world and make disciples (Matthew 28:19). They knew exactly what he was talking about. After spending more than three years with Jesus, they knew how to be fishers of men. They knew that to make disciples, they would need to teach God's Word and demonstrate its truth in real-life situations.

By God's grace, you and I will have about eighteen years of partnering with God to raise disciples who love him. If all we do is raise children who have memorized Bible stories but who fail to apply them to their own lives, we will have failed.

Brother, fall in love with Jesus with every ounce of your being. Study his Word and keep it close to your heart. Teach it to your kids every opportunity you get—when you're getting groceries, when you're throwing a baseball in the backyard, when you're eating dinner at a restaurant, and when you're hanging out at a barbecue with your neighbors. Keep your eyes open for any opportunity to point your children back to their Creator.

8

A CASE OF THE RONALDS

Create Gospel-Centered
Traditions and Memorials

My mom started taking my sisters and me to church when I was seven years old. I always enjoyed church but didn't fully count the cost of following Jesus until the summer between seventh and eighth grade. Until then, the innocence of childhood and the righteous life to which God was calling his followers seemed to blend together in my mind. The idea of conscious rebellion against the will of God hadn't occurred to me.

But in seventh grade, I was exposed to pornography at a friend's house. Seventh grade was the year my friends started having sex with their girlfriends. It was when my friends first got drunk and tried smoking weed. For the first time, I had to decide what I wanted to believe and what kind of life I wanted to live.

During a church camp that summer, I sat in the back of the room and told God I didn't want to live the way my friends did. Instead, I wanted to surrender my life and my desires to him.

When I returned home, I was determined to live out that decision in everyday life. Not really knowing where to begin, I figured the best place to start would be to serve the vulnerable and marginalized in my community. There was an assisted living facility across the street from my church, so I hopped on my bike and rode over to see how I could help.

When I walked into the building, the staff appeared confused to see me. I'm guessing not too many sweaty thirteen-year-old boys walk through their doors.

"Can I help you, sir?" the lady at the front desk asked.

"Yeah, I was hoping to find a place to volunteer. Do you have any volunteer opportunities here?" I asked.

Her look of confusion only grew more intense. "Umm...I think so. Let me think." She looked down at the floor for a solid thirty seconds. I could tell she was racking her brain to come up with something.

"Well, the residents can get pretty lonely around here. I'm sure they'd love playing board games with you. In fact, let me introduce you to Ronald—you two would get along great!" She walked me over to a sweet old man who was sitting by the fireplace in the lobby.

"Hi, Ronald, I'm Jerrad. Would you like to play checkers with me?" I asked.

"That would be just fine," he replied with a smile on his face.

We sat down at a table, and I began setting up the board to play. Once all the pieces were in place, I told Ronald he could go first. He made his first move and then looked at me, indicating that it was my turn.

I've always been a competitive guy, so I sat for a bit, pondering the most strategic first play. Apparently, in those twenty seconds, Ronald had forgotten whose turn it was. Without saying a word, he took another piece and moved for a second time.

I looked up at him with a puzzled expression on my face.

"Oh...actually, Ronald, it's my turn," I said.

"No, it's not," he said sternly.

I wasn't quite sure what to do next. I had never been in an argument with an elderly man. I decided to let this one slide and looked back down at the board, continuing to strategize.

Ten more seconds went by, and Ronald's hand moved back onto the board to move the third piece in a row.

"Um…Ronald, it's definitely my turn," I said sheepishly.

Without hesitating, Ronald stood up and flipped the entire board off the coffee table. "I've had enough of your cheating!" he shouted as he walked away.

I sat there in stunned silence.

The next day, I woke up and rode my bike back to the facility, eager to interact with more residents. As soon as I walked through the front doors, I found Ronald standing at the desk with a big smile on his face.

"There you are, Jerrad! I've been waiting for you since breakfast. Would you like to play checkers?"

"Sure," I said, laughing to myself.

Without fail, we were only three minutes into the game when Ronald again walked away angrily because he was convinced I was cheating. For the rest of the summer, I walked into the facility each morning to find Ronald anxiously awaiting my arrival.

"There you are, Jerrad! Up for a game of checkers?"

Every morning we played, and every morning he accused me of cheating. Ronald had a memory problem.

If you've ever walked through memory loss with a loved one, you know that it can be painful and that sometimes the only way to cope is to laugh. I often found myself laughing as Ronald accused me of cheating day after day.

SPIRITUAL DEMENTIA

This year Leila and I are reading through the Bible together. One thing that has stuck out to me is how many people in Scripture have a case of "the Ronalds." Despite how often God seems to show up in people's lives, they forget all too quickly.

Remember the story of God using Moses to rescue his people from slavery in Egypt?

The Israelites had been enslaved for four hundred years when Moses showed up to set them free. Pharaoh had been hard-hearted toward God and was determined not to let God's people go. So God, being God, decides to demonstrate his strength and sends ten plagues against Egypt. Pharaoh finally decides he's had enough.

The Israelites make a quick getaway, but Pharaoh has a change of heart and orders the Egyptian troops to chase after them. The Israelites are trapped between the soldiers and the Red Sea with nowhere to go, and they start freaking out on Moses: "It would have been better for us to serve the Egyptians than to die in the wilderness" (Exodus 14:12).

Moses, not really knowing what is going to happen but certain that God will make a way, tries to convince the people that everything will be okay.

What God does next is one of the most amazing miracles in Scripture.

God commands Moses to lift up his staff and says he will split the Red Sea in half, allowing the Israelites to walk through on dry ground and elude the Egyptian army.

Sure enough, God does exactly what he has promised, and the Israelites escape without a scratch. When they arrive on the other side of the sea, they do what any of us would do in that situation—they start thanking God. They pull out their tambourines and begin to sing and dance.

It's the first public worship service in the Bible.

Almost the entire chapter of Exodus 15 is filled with the Israelites' spontaneous worship in response to what God has just done for them. They passionately sing and dance for joy at God's goodness, his mercy, his salvation, his glory, and his majesty. They are convinced to the core that they serve the one true God, and they can't help but sing about his goodness.

And then they pull a Ronald.

Just three days after their giant worship service, they are walking through the desert and they get thirsty. They forget about God's goodness and miraculous provision, and they begin to grumble again. Before Exodus 15 even closes, the Israelites are right back to the same attitude they had before crossing the Red Sea.

As I reread their story, I was just as baffled as I had been the first time I met Ronald. How in the world could the Israelites forget about God's goodness in just a few days?

Fast-forward to the New Testament, and you'll find Jesus's disciples also struggling with their own version of spiritual dementia.

On one occasion, Jesus was teaching the crowds about the kingdom of God when they began to grow hungry. The disciples knew that there wasn't any food nearby and encouraged Jesus to send the masses home to get something to eat.

"You give them something to eat," Jesus tells them in Mark 6:37.

The disciples were confused. They hadn't brought enough food for five thousand men (plus their wives and children). And they knew Jesus hadn't either.

Jesus, being God, uses every possible situation to help grow his disciples' faith. Just as God miraculously saved the Israelites at the Red Sea, Jesus miraculously saves the people by providing food for the entire crowd. Everyone there must have been absolutely amazed.

Shortly after, Jesus repeats the same miracle with another crowd of four thousand.

On two separate occasions, Jesus encounters hungry crowds, and both times he miraculously provides for them.

God has a reputation
for taking care of
his people, and
we have a reputation
for forgetting
what he's done.

Again, the crowds and the disciples must have been absolutely amazed...until they pull a Ronald.

Listen to what takes place immediately after the second story of Jesus providing bread for a huge crowd. The disciples load up into a boat and make their way to the other side of the Sea of Galilee, and then this happens:

> Now they had forgotten to bring bread, and they had only one loaf with them in the boat. And he cautioned them, saying, "Watch out; beware of the leaven of the Pharisees and the leaven of Herod." And they began discussing with one another the fact that they had no bread. And Jesus, aware of this, said to them, "Why are you discussing the fact that you have no bread? Do you not yet perceive or understand? Are your hearts hardened? Having eyes do you not see, and having ears do you not hear? And do you not remember? When I broke the five loaves for the five thousand, how many baskets full of broken pieces did you take up?" They said to him, "Twelve." "And the seven for the four thousand, how many baskets full of broken pieces did you take up?" And they said to him, "Seven." And he said to them, "Do you not yet understand?" (Mark 8:14-21).

You can almost sense the frustration in Jesus's voice shouting from the text as he questions his disciples. They had seen him miraculously provide food for more than nine thousand people, and now the twelve of them were worried about lunch.

I can imagine Jesus grabbing them by the shoulders and saying, "Are you kidding me? Did you seriously forget what I *just did* for those crowds?"

God has a reputation for taking care of his people, and we have a reputation for forgetting what he's done.

WHAT VACATION?

If we're honest, we'll admit that when it comes to God's faithfulness, the Israelites and the disciples aren't the only ones who have memory issues.

It seems crazy to think that just three days after the giant worship service by the Red Sea, the Israelites go right back to their anxiety about how God will provide for them. And yet how many times have we been caught struggling in our faith just days after singing about God's goodness on a Sunday morning?

> **How many times have we been caught struggling in our faith just days after singing about God's goodness on a Sunday morning?**

Sometimes I don't even make it three days. Leila will tell you she's found me dealing with fear, anxiety, or doubt just three *hours* after leading thousands of people in worship. One hour I am convinced of who God is, and the next I forget what he has done.

If I'm not constantly reminded of God's reputation and character, I begin to drift toward sin, doubt, fear, and anxiety.

The worst part is that our children aren't immune to this issue of forgetfulness.

Every year, I plan a big trip for our family to explore a new part of the country. At the beginning of this year, I took our whole squad across the country to visit Florida. None of us had been before, and being from Oregon, we'd heard rumors that they have this big, hot, glowing ball in the sky called the sun.

We spent the week swimming in the ocean, visiting friends, boating among dolphins, screaming down giant waterslides, and getting sunburned beyond belief. It was epic—by far one of the most fun family vacations we've had.

The other night at dinner, I asked our kids what their favorite part of the trip was.

"What trip?" they said.

"The Florida trip. Eight months ago. The one where we counted down for almost half a year in excitement. The one where you swam in the ocean for the first time. The one where you flew down the waterslides. The one where we watched dolphins jump right in front of our eyes!"

"Oh, yeah. I don't really remember much about it," Elijah said.

I almost flipped the dinner table the same way Ronald flipped that checkerboard.

"How in the world could you forget so quickly?" I asked.

"I don't know…it seems like forever ago."

I pulled out my phone and started showing them pictures of the vacation, hoping to jostle their memories. As I swiped from photo to photo, they slowly started to remember the details of the trip and began to share some of their favorite memories from it.

> **If I'm not constantly reminded of God's reputation and character, I begin to drift toward sin, doubt, fear, and anxiety.**

Had I not taken the pictures, I'm not sure they would have even remembered that they went.

Here's the sad truth: If I don't remind them often about what we've done as a family, they will forget about it. And if I don't remind them often about Jesus, they will forget about him too. Left to ourselves, we don't drift toward God—we drift away from him. Our sin nature, given to us at birth, pulls us away from the things of God, not toward them.

Just as my kids needed to see the photos on my phone to jostle their memories of a great vacation, we need constant reminders that will point us and our children back toward our great God.

DRY GROUND

Let's take a minute and go back to that story of the Israelites being rescued from slavery.

If you fast-forward almost forty years to the day, you'll find that Moses has died and God has given the Israelites a new young leader named Joshua. After forty long years of wandering in the desert, they are finally coming to the end of their journey.

> **If I don't remind them often about Jesus, they will forget about him too. Left to ourselves, we don't drift toward God—we drift away from him.**

And once again, they are faced with a water dilemma. But instead of having to cross the Red Sea, they must cross the Jordan River to enter the Promised Land.

God commanded Joshua to have a leader from every tribe come and stand on the banks of the Jordan while holding the Ark of the Covenant (which was where God dwelled among them). When they did, God made the waters stop upriver, allowing the Israelites to walk through safely on dry ground.

Forty years earlier, the Israelites entered a new season by walking through water on dry ground. Now that season ended as they again walked through water on dry ground to the land God had promised them.

But this time, God makes sure they won't have another case of the Ronalds. Listen to what he instructs them to do when they get to the other side of the river:

> When all the nation had finished passing over the Jordan, the LORD said to Joshua, "Take twelve men from the people, from each tribe a man, and command them, saying, 'Take twelve stones from here out of the midst of the Jordan, from the very place where the priests' feet stood firmly, and bring them over with you and lay them down in the place where you lodge tonight.'" Then Joshua called the twelve men from the people of Israel, whom he had appointed, a

man from each tribe. And Joshua said to them, "Pass on before the ark of the LORD your God into the midst of the Jordan, and take up each of you a stone upon his shoulder, according to the number of the tribes of the people of Israel, that this may be a sign among you. When your children ask in time to come, 'What do those stones mean to you?' then you shall tell them that the waters of the Jordan were cut off before the ark of the covenant of the LORD. When it passed over the Jordan, the waters of the Jordan were cut off. So these stones shall be to the people of Israel a memorial forever…"

> **Just as my kids needed to see photos to jostle their memories of a great vacation, we need constant reminders that will point us and our children back toward our great God.**

And those twelve stones, which they took out of the Jordan, Joshua set up at Gilgal. And he said to the people of Israel, "When your children ask their fathers in times to come, 'What do these stones mean?' then you shall let your children know, 'Israel passed over this Jordan on dry ground.' For the LORD your God dried up the waters of the Jordan for you until you passed over, as the LORD your God did to the Red Sea, which he dried up for us until we passed over, so that all the peoples of the earth may know that the hand of the LORD is mighty, that you may fear the LORD your God forever" (Joshua 4:1-7,20-24).

Catch this: Before God allows them to take one more step toward the Promised Land, he commands them to build a visual monument to remind them of God's faithfulness for generations to come. He knows their reputation for forgetfulness and wants to make sure they remember what he's done.

Remember the verse that opened chapter 7? Read it again, but this time notice what God says about creating visual reminders.

These words that I command you today shall be on your heart. You shall teach them diligently to your children, and shall talk of them when you sit in your house, and when you walk by the way, and when you lie down, and when you rise. You shall bind them as a sign on your hand, and they shall be as frontlets between your eyes. You shall write them on the doorposts of your house and on your gates (Deuteronomy 6:6-9).

God seems to be aware that if we aren't constantly reminding ourselves and our children of who he is and what he has done, we are prone to forget.

Build a memorial for your kids to see.

Write it on the doorposts of your house and on your gates.

There is something powerful about creating a visual reminder to point us back to God.

SEEK FIRST

Leila and I had been married only a short time when I started struggling with something new—bouts of depression and anxiety. I had zero track record of these things in my past, so I wasn't sure what to make of it. I was losing sleep and dealing with other physical symptoms. I went to a doctor to see what was going on, and he asked, "Is there something bothering you?"

"I don't think so," I said.

And I wasn't lying. I had just married the girl of my dreams. We had bought a new house. We had just adopted a cute little puppy. I had a really great job at a wonderful church. I was living the American dream.

But something wasn't settled deep in my soul. God was quietly nudging me and trying to get my attention.

I asked Leila to join me in prayer, and we began to seek God together over a period of several months.

As time passed, it became clearer and clearer to me that I needed to step

If we aren't
constantly reminding
ourselves and our
children of who
God is and what he
has done, we are
prone to forget.

out of my role on the pastoral staff of our church. I hadn't had any big personal issues, and I enjoyed my job. In fact, I was doing well and constantly being affirmed by those around me. But I knew deep in my heart that God was calling me to something else.

I needed to find the courage to talk to Leila about what I was feeling. To be honest, I was slightly terrified. Leila isn't an emotional decision-maker. She is wise and grounded in facts. She plays out every scenario in her head and evaluates all the consequences. I knew she'd immediately come back with questions:

"What do you feel God is calling you to instead?"

"If you quit, how will we cover our new mortgage and all our bills?"

"Are you sure this is God speaking to you and not the lunch you just ate?"

Honestly, I didn't have good answers to any of those questions. I had no idea what God was calling me to do after I quit. I didn't know any of the next steps. I just knew that step one was to quit my current job.

I also had no idea how we would cover the mortgage or pay our bills. My quitting would mean us losing 50 percent of our income, and that certainly wouldn't allow us to maintain our home or lifestyle.

I spent an entire day praying about having that conversation with her and finally mustered up the courage to talk when she got home from work one night.

"Hey, babe, I think God might be calling me to quit my job," I said quietly, looking at the floor.

"Yeah, I think so too. I'm not sure why, but I've been sensing the same thing in my spirit."

Wait—what?

I was totally caught off guard. I had prepared a long speech with bullet points for all my counterarguments. I wasn't prepared for this.

She walked across the kitchen and gave me a big hug. "I'm willing to follow Jesus with you, wherever he might lead us."

At that moment, I was reminded of the verse that says, "He who finds a wife finds a good thing and obtains favor from the Lord" (Proverbs 18:22).

The next morning, I walked into our senior pastor's office, sat down, and told him I needed to leave.

He was completely unprepared for this. "Where are you going?"

"I'm not sure. Leila and I just sense that this is what God is calling us to do."

He spent the next hour encouraging me, praying over me, and asking permission to join me in the process of seeking God together for whatever this next season would hold. I walked out of his office with a sense of relief and excitement about what God was going to do next.

When I got home, Leila and I spent some time talking and dreaming about the future. We were scared out of our minds because we had no idea where God would lead us, but we felt a deep sense of peace because even though we didn't know where we were going, we knew who was going with us.

I went to sleep that night with more excitement in my heart than I had felt in a long time…until 4:30 a.m.

Leila woke up early to get ready for work. When she came back into the room, she turned on the lights and gently pushed on my shoulder. Rubbing my eyes, I tried to make sense of what was going on. She nervously smiled and began to hand me something I didn't recognize. At first I thought it was a thermometer, which confused me because I wasn't sick. When I looked more closely, I saw it had two solid lines.

"We're having a baby!" she said with tears in her eyes.

Without even thinking, the first words that popped out of my mouth were "Oh, crap. I just quit my job."

Turns out those aren't the first words your wife wants to hear when she finds out she's pregnant with your first child. I apologized and hugged her, and we laughed together, sitting on the bed in total shock.

What began as excitement for the next season of life quickly turned into fear. I started to doubt everything I'd sensed that God had been telling me over the previous months.

Was that really God talking to me?

If so, why would he have me quit my job right before we have a baby?

Is it too late to ask for my job back?

Providing as a husband is one thing—providing as a dad is something else altogether!

My feelings of anxiety multiplied. I was more anxious than ever.

I called a friend and asked if we could grab lunch so I could tell him what was going on. I spent the entire time explaining all my doubts about what I thought I'd heard God say and how nervous I was to bring a new baby into our lives without a job.

"Jerrad, your only job is to seek Jesus. He'll take care of the rest. Go home and memorize what Jesus said in Matthew 6:33-34," he said.

When I got home, I pulled out my Bible and opened it to the verse in Matthew that my friend had encouraged me to remember.

> Seek first the kingdom of God and his righteousness, and all these things will be added to you…Do not be anxious about tomorrow, for tomorrow will be anxious for itself. Sufficient for the day is its own trouble (Matthew 6:33-34).

I had read this verse a thousand times, but the truth of the promise had never been more real to me than it was in that moment. It wasn't just something nice Jesus said to some disciples; it was my only source of hope in a very scary season.

I immediately jumped on my laptop and typed the verse into a blank document.

Print. Quantity: 50.

I spent the next thirty minutes taping copies of the verse throughout my house. You couldn't walk two feet without seeing it somewhere. The microwave, refrigerator, mirrors, bathroom, and garage doors…you name it, I taped the verse on it.

When friends came over, they made fun of me. "Nice decoration. What's this all about?"

"I have a tendency to forget who God is and what he's done. So I put these up everywhere to remind me of his faithfulness," I'd tell them.

I knew that like the Israelites crossing the Jordan River, I would need to build a memorial to remind me, Leila, and our future children of the kind of God we serve.

I knew that if I wasn't reminded every few feet of God's character, I'd be prone to forget. And I didn't want to pull a Ronald.

I wanted to remember.

A HOME WITH INTENTION

More than seven years have passed since that season of life, and to this day, whenever I read Jesus's words in Matthew 6, I am reminded that my only job is to seek first his kingdom, and he will take care of everything else.

We ended up losing our new house because we couldn't pay the mortgage. We sold our cars and just about everything else we owned to make ends meet. It was one of the hardest times we have ever gone through, and yet one of the most spiritually rewarding.

Matthew 6 will always stand as a memorial and a testament to God's goodness in our lives.

I've spent the last eight years trying to build as many memorials as I can. Today, if you were to walk into our home, almost everything you'd see has been intentionally placed there as a memorial to remind our family of who God is and what he has done.

I have a long way to go when it comes to being the kind of spiritual leader my family needs, but one thing I'm glad I've done is create an environment in my home that helps me talk to my kids about Jesus on a regular basis.

Every home and every family will be different. What was a significant memorial to the Israelites was just a pile of rocks to someone else passing by. But that pile of rocks represented God's miraculous provision for generations to come.

I'm going to list some of my family's rhythms and traditions. These are things we do regularly to help us remember who God is. My hope is to get your creative juices flowing, and I encourage you to steal some of these for yourself. But more importantly, I encourage you to sit down as a family and create custom memorials to celebrate the unique ways God has shown up for you. By God's grace, they will serve as a reminder of God's goodness to your family for generations to come.

BUILDING MEMORIALS

Our Vase

At the beginning of each year, we set an empty vase on top of the fireplace mantle with a stack of scratch paper next to it. Throughout the year, whenever we see God move, we write a quick note about it and place it into the vase. Sometimes we write about the amazing sunset we saw out the front window. Sometimes we thank God for new friends or neighbors. Sometimes we thank God for meeting a financial or practical need. There are no rules—we simply write down anything that comes to mind when we think about how God showed up that day. At the end of the year, we spend time as a family reading through each note and reflecting on how good God has been to us over the past year. The vase and the notes inside act as a memorial to remind us how often God shows up in both big and small ways throughout the year.

A Photo Wall

Several years ago we set a goal to have a hundred people share a meal in our home within one year. We invited friends, coworkers, neighbors, and sometimes strangers to join us for dinner. Regardless of how long each meal lasted, our hope was always that when our guests left our home, they would find themselves a little closer to Jesus than when they first arrived. At the end of each meal, we used a Polaroid camera to take a picture with our guests and then hung the photo on the wall.

When someone comes to our house for the first time, they usually stand in front of the photo wall and look at each picture. The wall acts as a memorial, helping our family and our guests remember that God is working beyond our individual lives to redeem the entire world back to himself.

An Empty Plate

At many of our dinners, we set an empty plate at the table to remind us of two things: first, that some people go hungry every day and that God wants to use us to bring his kingdom to the poor and vulnerable, and second, that God has blessed us to be a blessing. So the empty plate reminds us to think about who we could invite over to join us for a meal and share our lives. It serves as a memorial to my kids that God has met our needs and that he desires to use us to meet the needs of others.

Making the Bed

In her book *Liturgy of the Ordinary*, author Tish Harrison Warren describes how the simplest of tasks can be acts of worship. Based on her advice, I started a new tradition of making my bed first thing in the morning. As I straighten the messy blankets, I am reminded of how God takes broken and messy things and makes them new. Sometimes I invite my kids to join me. I often open a Bible app and read Scripture for a few minutes after I fix the bed, or I ask God to take the broken and messy areas of my life and make them knew. Every time I walk into my room and see my made bed, I remember that God is true to his promise to clean up what our sin has broken.

Framed Vows

As we talked about in chapter 2, your marriage is one of the main tools God uses to help shape your life to look more like his. I want to see my marriage not as a burden but as an instrument in my sanctification. To help me constantly remember this, I've printed our wedding vows, framed them, and hung them prominently in the main hallway. I walk past those vows several times a day and am reminded of the covenant and commitment I made with my wife. The framed vows act as a memorial to remind me to pursue my wife with the same relentless love with which Christ pursued me.

Candlelit Dinners

On a recent *Dad Tired* podcast, author Andy Crouch shared about his recent book *A Tech-Wise Family*, in which he helps families put technology in its proper place. He mentioned that his family spends many nights sharing candlelit dinners. In an age of constant screens, this idea was extremely appealing to me. Based on his suggestion, our family now enjoys many of our meals by candlelight. As we sit around the table together and watch the flickering of the flames, we are reminded to pause and celebrate moments of Sabbath each day. The candles act as subtle visual reminders that resting in the Lord and enjoying the company of those around us is worth more than anything we can accomplish through work or social media.

These are just a few of the things we do regularly as a family to help us remember who we are in Christ and what he has done for us. As the spiritual leader of your home, you can give your family a tremendous gift by finding practical ways to constantly point them toward Jesus.

FORGETTING FIRST GEAR

When I was sixteen years old and had just gotten my driver's license, I asked my mom if I could borrow her car.

"You don't know how to drive a stick shift," she said.

"Give me ten minutes. I'll watch a YouTube video and learn everything I need to know."

Ten minutes later, I went back into the living room and asked for her keys.

She was incredulous. "Are you serious?" she asked.

"Absolutely. I got this."

I hopped in the car and drove to the nearest grocery store to pick up some soda and snacks.

> Forgetting the faithfulness of God, even in the small things, will lead to a life full of fear, anxiety, arrogance, and sin.

After grabbing everything I needed, I walked out of the store and into the parking lot to load up. There was just one major problem.

The car was missing.

You have to be kidding me. Did someone really steal my car? I was only gone five minutes!

I stood in shock, my hands full of groceries, scanning the parking lot and hoping to find some clues.

In the distance I could see something abnormal toward the back of the lot. I squinted my eyes and made my way closer.

"What the heck?" I said to myself out loud.

As I got closer to the back of the parking lot, I saw my mom's car sitting empty, smashed into another parked vehicle.

It turns out that I'd forgotten one small but crucial detail when parking the car. When I pulled into the parking spot, I'd left it in neutral instead of shifting into first. As I walked into the store, the car was slowly rolling away behind me, headed directly toward the other parked cars behind it.

I felt like an absolute idiot. I had forgotten one small step, and it cost me (and my mom's insurance company) dearly.

Brother, this whole memorial thing is bigger than stacking rocks or filling vases with scratch paper. If you fail to remember who God is and what he has done, you will inevitably lose track of your spiritual life and turn around only to find it smashed. Forgetting the faithfulness of God, even in the small things, will lead to a life full of fear, anxiety, arrogance, and sin.

Don't pull a Ronald. Don't let your kids develop spiritual dementia. Write about the things of God on your doorposts and on your gates. Put up an empty vase, light some candles, make the bed, stack some rocks. Just do whatever it takes to remember who this God is that you serve.

9

HEADED TO ASPEN

Everyone Is Busy, but Few Are Intentional

One of my all-time favorite movies is *Dumb and Dumber*, starring Jim Carey and Jeff Daniels. It's one of the few movies I've watched countless times, and I've memorized nearly every line. As a pastor, I really shouldn't recommend it, but if you need another movie to add to your watch list...

In case you haven't already seen it, the plot revolves around two best friends, Lloyd and Harry, who haven't quite developed the skills to make it in life. They're single, can't keep a job, and have no money. Before being fired, Lloyd was a limo driver and Harry was a pet groomer.

On one of Lloyd's last trips as a driver, he drives an attractive woman to the airport but later realizes she boarded the plane without her briefcase. In an act of spontaneity, the two friends decide to drop what little they have going for them and drive across the country to return the missing item.

In one scene of their road trip, Harry is passed out in the passenger's seat when Lloyd looks over at him and plugs his friend's nose. While Lloyd is busy trying to be funny, he misses his turnoff and ends up driving in the wrong direction. The next scene shows the pair in the middle of Lincoln, Nebraska, more than six hundred miles from their intended destination of

Aspen, Colorado. In one of the funniest scenes in the movie, the two realize what a giant mistake they've made and begin to argue.

BIRTHDAY CAKE

I've spent the past thirteen years in ministry, often meeting with men who tell me they are far from where they want to be in life. They feel frustrated with the apathy they feel toward the things of God, the way their marriages have declined over the years, and the kinds of fathers they are turning out to be.

In their minds, they were headed toward Aspen, Colorado, but somehow ended up in Lincoln, Nebraska. No offense to Lincoln, Nebraska—it's just not where they imagined they would be. These men are often dissatisfied with their lives and have no idea how they got to where they currently are.

Last week I had lunch with one of my best friends, Dan. We've gone through much of life together, and we try to constantly encourage each other to be the man, husband, and father God has called us to be. During lunch, he shared honestly about a time in his marriage when he felt like he was missing the mark and he didn't quite know where he'd gone wrong.

He was a real estate agent, working twelve to fourteen hours a day, six or seven days a week, and was burning the candle at both ends. His marriage was in a rough spot. He told me that during that season, he and his wife would have both admitted that they felt more like roommates than partners in ministry and life.

Although he knew it was bad, he justified being a workaholic by telling himself that he was doing what any man should do—working as hard as he could to provide for his family.

The week of his daughter's second birthday, his wife asked him to pick up a birthday cake from Costco for the party that Saturday. "I know you're busy and have a lot going on, but can you please remember to do this? It's important to me," she told him.

He agreed to the task and added it to his already full to-do list for the week.

On Friday night, he woke up in a panic from a dead sleep. *Oh, crap! I forgot to pick up the cake!*

He quietly escaped from the bedroom and went downstairs to bake a cake of his own.

He started pulling out all the ingredients from the shelves, determined to make a birthday cake for his daughter that his wife would be proud of. Or at least one she wouldn't kill him over.

As he reached inside the refrigerator to grab some eggs, he looked down and saw a birthday cake from Costco sitting on the bottom shelf. He stood in his kitchen alone in the middle of the night and started bawling.

"Jerrad, I wept," he told me. "I just couldn't believe how I had gotten here as a husband and dad. I didn't want to suck. I didn't want to be far from my wife and kids. I didn't wake up one day and say I would just check out. It had been a slow fade, and it finally caught up to me. Seeing that birthday cake reminded me that this isn't the kind of man I want to be, and I knew something needed to change."

I don't think my friend Dan is alone in this feeling. In fact, I don't have a single friend who is making a conscious decision to be a crappy husband and father. I interact with the guys of the Dad Tired community every day, and I feel confident saying that none of them woke up one morning and decided they would just give up.

Like Dan said, it's a slow fade. It's one small decision after another, day after day, that leads us to Nebraska.[1]

---

[1]   Seriously, I'm sorry, Nebraska. I'm sure you're awesome. But you get the point I'm trying to make.

HOW DID I GET HERE?

A few years ago, Leila wanted to go to the mall to pick out a new outfit and asked me to join her. I'm not a huge fan of the mall, but I am a huge fan of my wife, so I agreed to tag along. A few minutes into our trip, I started to experience a serious case of SLS (shopping leg syndrome). It's a disease I discovered and diagnosed myself, but I've been encouraged to know I'm not alone. Many of my married friends also regularly suffer from the condition.

"Hey, babe, would it be okay if I went to look at some guy stuff?" I asked.

"Have fun," she said with a smile.

I had noticed a Harley-Davidson dealership on the other side of the parking lot. I decided it'd be fun to check out some motorcycles while my wife tried on some clothes.

"Can I help you, sir?" a bearded, tattooed man asked as I walked in the front doors.

"Nah. I'm good, dude. I'm just looking around."

"Why don't I walk with you?"

I have a reputation for getting into deep conversations quickly with strangers, so somehow I immediately hit it off with this sixty-five-year-old man who looks nothing like me. We walked around the store together, sharing stories and making each other laugh.

Forty-five minutes later—and I kid you not—I was signing the paperwork to my very first Harley-Davidson motorcycle.

I have never ridden a motorcycle. I don't have a motorcycle endorsement. I couldn't afford a motorcycle. And knowing me, I would have crashed this one before I reached the other side of the parking lot.

But to my surprise, I was buying a motorcycle that day. This guy had completely blindsided me. I didn't even see it coming![2]

---

[2]   Yes, that's a *Dumb and Dumber* reference. Good catch.

One bonus of buying a motorcycle that day was a free $200 gift card to the Harley-Davidson apparel store. Before completing the paperwork fully, I headed over to their clothing section and began trying on new leather jackets.

I looked down at my phone and saw a text from Leila. "Hey, babe, I'm all done shopping. Where are you?"

"I'm at the Harley dealership across the parking lot."

"???" she responded.

A few minutes later, she walked through the front door of the dealership. I was wearing a helmet and leather jacket when she saw me.

"What's going on here?" She was laughing.

"Hey, babe, I just bought a new Harley!"

She laughed even more.

"No, I'm serious! Mike over there convinced me to pull the trigger."

No more laughter.

We spent the next twenty-five minutes going back and forth about my decision before I sheepishly walked over to my new friend Mike and told him I had to cancel the deal.

Thankfully, Leila was able to talk some sense into me before I signed my life away (maybe literally). She reminded me where we were in our lives and where we dreamed about going in the future, and she showed me that my decision to buy a motorcycle didn't fit with those goals.

I look back at that day and can't help but laugh. How in the world did I end up in a Harley-Davidson store, signing the papers to a motorcycle? I didn't have any intention of buying a bike when I woke up that morning. How did I get there?

ADDICTED TO BUSY

When was the last time you asked someone how they were doing and they responded with "focused" or "intentional"?

If you heard someone say that, you'd probably think they'd fallen off their rocker and needed to be checked into a mental facility.

I never hear people talk about how intentional or focused they are with their lives. Instead, I hear one word over and over when I sit down and ask people how they are doing: "busy."

All of us are busy, yet few of us know why or where we're trying to go.

> **We're addicted to busyness.**

Whenever I hang out with people, I have an ongoing bet with myself to see what they will say when I ask them how they are doing. Nine times out of ten, they say the word "busy" in the first few sentences.

We're addicted to busyness.

I was recently a guest on a podcast where the host asked me how I'm able to manage my time effectively. "Jerrad, I know you're so busy running a ministry, writing books, and hosting a podcast. How do you manage to find the time to be an intentional husband and dad in the middle of all that?"

"I'm really good at saying no," I told him.

He laughed.

"I'm serious, bro. I say no to just about everything so I can say yes to the few things that matter."

Last week I was at a birthday party for one of Eden's friends and was talking to another dad.

"How have you been, man?" I asked as I ate way too much of the pizza and cake meant for the kids.

"Good, dude. Busy. Every day is nuts. We're dropping kids off at school, then ballet, then soccer practice, then trying to bathe them and feed them as quickly as possible before bed. We wake up and start the whole thing over again. It's crazy."

I was exhausted just listening to his weekly schedule. I imagined a car driving down the freeway and pulling off at every exit to see what it had to offer. Yes, the car was moving forward, but was it really going anywhere? Would it ever reach its intended destination? Did it even know what the final destination was?

Just because you're driving doesn't mean you know where you're going. And just because you're busy doesn't mean you're intentional.

Have you ever stopped to ask yourself why you're so busy?

When guys meet with me to tell me they're having a hard time balancing life and work and their relationship with Jesus, I often ask them to try a simple exercise: Spend one day this week tracking what you do every ten minutes from 8:00 a.m. to 8:00 p.m.

You'll be amazed at what you spend time doing.

Most guys come back a week later and tell me they didn't really have a time issue—they had an intentionality issue. They were saying yes to everything without fully knowing why.

As Leila and I are reading through the Bible together this year, one thing that really sticks out to me is how little time Jesus spent healing people.

> **Just because you're driving doesn't mean you know where you're going. And just because you're busy doesn't mean you're intentional.**

When the God of the universe showed up in flesh in blood, he could have healed thousands of people en masse, and yet we see him perform only a handful of healings, one by one.

Why didn't he put on healing revivals where people could line up for a healing touch from Jesus? Why did Jesus spend only three and a half years

When we don't
have a clear goal
of where we are
trying to go,
life and people have
a way of trying
to figure that out
for us.

in ministry? Couldn't he have walked around until he was ninety, healing as many people as possible?

Jesus was good at saying no. He even said no to spending more time healing people. Why? Because he knew he needed to say yes to something much bigger.

Jesus didn't come just to heal sick people for a few years. He came to heal the brokenness of our world for all time. His purpose wasn't to perform a few miracles for a select few. His purpose was to perform the miracle of reconciling all of humanity back to himself once and for all.

Jesus said no to a lot of things, even good things, so he could say yes to the greatest thing.

Imagine how frustrated the disciples might have felt, knowing all the power that Jesus possessed but seeing how seldom he used it. But if Jesus wasn't intentional about his time, if he wasn't clear about why he came and where he was going, other people would have found a purpose for him.

> **Jesus was good at saying no.**

When we don't have a clear goal of where we are trying to go, life and people have a way of trying to figure that out for us. We end up saying yes to everything—many of them, good things—because we aren't totally clear what we're supposed to say no to. Without the destination in mind, we find ourselves pulling off at every exit.

I think for most guys, the problem isn't necessarily that they are in Nebraska but instead that they never knew they were trying to get to Aspen.

Here's what I mean: It's hard to know you're lost if you don't know where you're trying to get to in the first place. Why were Harry and Lloyd upset they were in Nebraska? Not because Nebraska was bad. They were upset because they knew it wasn't their destination.

My friend Dan wasn't upset that he was working too hard—working hard isn't necessarily wrong. He was upset because his working too hard was moving him away from his destination of being the husband and father God desired him to be.

Take a minute right now and ask yourself, *Where am I trying to go? What's my destination?*

> **It's hard to know you're lost if you don't know where you're trying to get to in the first place.**

I'm not referring to your career goals or your financial objectives. Rather, at the end of your life, when you're in your final days, what do you want to have accomplished as a man of God? What do you want your legacy to be?

That's your Aspen.

Because here's the truth: When you don't know what your priorities are, everything becomes a priority. And when you don't know what your Aspen is, everyone will tell you to head to theirs.

DRIFTING OFF TO SEA

Leila and I went to Hawaii for our honeymoon. When we arrived and got settled into the hotel, we went straight down to explore the beach just outside our room. Holding hands and looking into the crystal-clear water, we immediately spotted a group of giant sea turtles. I absolutely freaked out.

"I have to get in there!" I said like a six-year-old boy stumbling across a candy store.

I ran down to the local supermarket, grabbed a cheap pair of snorkeling goggles, and immediately went back down to the beach. I was gone less than twenty minutes.

When I returned to the hotel, Leila said, "I'm sorry, babe. They seemed to have swum off somewhere else."

"Darn it! Well, now that I have these goggles, I'll go in anyway and look around."

I took off my shirt and dove into the warm water.

I aimlessly floated with my head down for about thirty minutes, looking all around for the sea turtles. I finally decided I should probably spend more time with my new bride than chasing sea creatures.

When I finally popped my head out of the water, my heart sank. I had drifted hundreds of yards from the beach and could barely see the shore. It was at that moment that I realized how much I hate snorkeling.

> **When you don't know what your priorities are, everything becomes a priority.**

There was nothing but water surrounding me in every direction, and I could only imagine the school of sharks below me drawing straws to take the first bite of my scrawny little legs.

I was very far from where I wanted to be. How did I get there?

I didn't really know where I wanted to go when I jumped into the ocean that day, but I knew for a fact I didn't want to be where I ended up.

Maybe you feel as if you don't know where you're trying to go in life, and you aren't satisfied with where you've ended up. Maybe you feel busy but not intentional. You're constantly moving but not sure where you're headed.

A BROKEN GPS

Right after high school, a buddy and I decided to take a road trip across the country together. We had some friends who had moved to Kansas and needed to get their car back to the West Coast, so we offered to help by book-ing a one-way ticket to Kansas City and planned to make the long drive back to California.

In those days, we didn't have smartphones, so we were stuck with printed maps. I had heard about GPS devices you could install in your car. I'm a tech junkie, so I figured it was the perfect time to invest in the cutting-edge gadget.

So I bought a GPS that suctioned to the windshield of our car and tracked our every mile. We were absolutely amazed by the technology.

Somewhere between Colorado and Nevada, the sweet robotic voice of the GPS unit said, "In 268 miles, make a U-turn."

We burst into laughter. "What in the world?!" I said to my buddy, who was driving.

"Either the GPS has a glitch in the technology, or we are seriously off track," he said.

We pulled over at the next gas station to get some directions.

We discovered that the GPS unit had messed up our original coordinates, and we were more than two hundred miles from where we were supposed to be. What had started out as something funny turned into something incred-ibly frustrating.

We sat quietly in the car, not sure what to do.

"Well, that sucks. Let's grab a bag of Doritos and get back at it," I said.

We walked back into the gas station, grabbed some snacks, filled the car up with gas, and started our journey back to California.

Here's the thing: It's one thing to know you're not anywhere near where you want to be. It's another thing altogether to start making your way back to where you want to go.

Maybe you're starting to feel discouraged that you aren't the man God has called you to be. Maybe you're confused about where you are and where you should be going. Maybe the GPS just shouted at you to make a U-turn.

You have two options. You can sit in the car and be mad that you're so off base. Or you can grab a freaking bag of Doritos and get back at it.

You're off track. We've all been off track. Let's start the car back up and begin moving forward.

EVERYTHING IS MEANINGLESS

When I was in my midtwenties and newly married, I was really stressing out about what I should be doing with my life. I felt unsettled as a member of the pastoral staff of the church where I was working, and I was constantly anxious about my future. I remember calling a mentor and asking for some advice. He said something like this.

> Jerrad, knowing you and your personality, you will likely have a million job titles before you die. Jobs come and go. Business cards and titles will fade. At the end of the day, any employee can be replaced by someone else. But you know what can't be replaced? Your titles of husband, father, and disciple. These are the titles that will go with you to your grave. Stop stressing about what your career holds. Careers come and go. Focus on what you know God has called you to. You are a disciple of Jesus. You are a husband to Leila. You are a father to your children. Go home and do great at that.

This was one of the most life-defining conversations I have ever had. The Spirit of God spoke through my mentor and directly into my heart. He used my mentor to free me from the distractions that were holding me back and allowed me to focus on what God was calling me to.

Brother, my prayer for you is that this will be a life-defining moment for you as well. My prayer is that God will free you from the distractions, both good and bad, that are sidetracking you from your calling as a faithful disciple, husband, and father.

Jobs will come and go. Fantasy football leagues will come and go. Toys, gadgets, and new homes and cars will come and go. Your bank account will come and go. It's all fleeting. As the book of Ecclesiastes says when referring to the things of this world,

> "Meaningless! Meaningless!"
> says the Teacher.
> "Utterly meaningless!
> Everything is meaningless" (1:2 NIV).

Or as Jesus says,

> Do not lay up for yourselves treasures on earth, where moth and rust destroy and where thieves break in and steal, but lay up for yourselves treasures in heaven, where neither moth nor rust destroys and where thieves do not break in and steal (Matthew 6:19-21).

Laying treasures in heaven means loving the Lord your God with every ounce of your being. It means waking up every morning and loving your wife the same way Christ loved you. It means faithfully pursuing the hearts of your children the same way God continues to faithfully pursue your heart.

Brothers, this is your Aspen. This is the destination we are called to as men of God.

FINDING YOUR ASPEN

I want to walk you through a practical exercise to help you find your Aspen. This will be one of the most important pieces of this book, so please don't skip it.

Take out a blank piece of paper and draw three columns. In the first column, write the word "Disciple." In the second column, write the word "Husband." And in the third column, write the word "Father." In each row, write the numbers 10, 20, and 30.

DISCIPLE	HUSBAND	FATHER
10	10	10
20	20	20
30	30	30

Now, next to each number in every column, begin to describe your vision for where you want to be as a disciple, husband, and father. Where do you dream to be as a dad in the next ten years? What would you like to accomplish as a husband in the next ten years? Where would you like to be in your relationship with God ten years from now? Use as much detail as you can, and don't think about how things currently are or why those things aren't possible right now. Instead, think about how they could and should be. Dream big!

What about twenty years from now? And thirty? Take your time on this exercise. It will become the destination on your GPS for life.

Now that you've described in detail what your Aspen looks like in each of the unique roles God has called you to as a man of faith, it's time for you to ask yourself a very important question: *Why is this so important to me?*

Here's the truth: If you don't take the time to understand why these roles are so important to you, this will simply become an exercise that enters one ear and goes out the other. When the storms of life show up (and they most certainly will), you will become susceptible to drifting away from your Aspen. Your motivation shouldn't be the goals themselves but rather the "why" behind them. That's what allows you to wake up each morning and continue to chase your destination even when you're exhausted and Dad Tired. It's the "why" that gives you the courage to have hard conversations, to step into painful situations, and to say no to everything else fighting for your attention.

Brother, listen carefully. Your "why" is what reminds you to choose Aspen over Nebraska when everything inside of you is screaming, "Go to Nebraska! Just this one time. No one will know you took a quick side trip."

If you take the time to fully understand where you want to be as a man of God, and more importantly, why this is meaningful to you, you will sit on your deathbed when this short life passes by and utter the words of Paul with great joy: "I have fought the good fight, I have finished the race, I have kept the faith" (2 Timothy 4:7).

DO YOU WANT TO LEAVE TOO?

There is a passage in John where Jesus had been healing the sick and feeding the hungry. At this point in his ministry, the crowds gathered around him by the thousands. Everyone wanted to hear Jesus's words and see the miraculous signs he could perform.

If Jesus were like most of us, he would have been stoked that so many people were following him. Most of us judge the quality of our churches and ministries based on how many people are attending, and his ministry was growing tremendously. By our standards, he was a huge success.

But Jesus wasn't looking for numbers. He was looking for hearts. Success to him was based not on how many people he could get to show up but on how many people would give up their lives to follow him.

Jesus didn't want followers who were looking for miracles and bread. He wanted followers who were looking for sacrifice and service.

So Jesus, being Jesus, decides to up the cost of what it means to be his

Jesus wasn't
looking for
numbers.
He was looking
for hearts.

disciple. He begins to preach about *that* instead of about looking for bread in the desert as the Israelites did. Or about hoping to get fed with a couple of loaves and fish. He begins to preach that *he* is the bread of life they must eat.

> This is the bread that comes down from heaven, so that one may eat of it and not die. I am the living bread that came down from heaven. If anyone eats of this bread, he will live forever. And the bread that I will give for the life of the world is my flesh (John 6:50-51).

> **Jesus didn't want followers who were looking for miracles and bread. He wanted followers who were looking for sacrifice and service.**

For many in the audience, this was the final straw. They liked the Jesus who fed the hungry, healed the sick, calmed the storms, and preached a good message. But this whole "eat my flesh" thing was a little much. They wanted to follow Jesus, but in their minds, he had crossed a line, and they weren't willing to follow.

Feed the hungry? Absolutely.

Heal the sick? All for it.

Show off some miracles? Definitely.

Eat your flesh? Not a chance.

Listen to what they do next: "After this many of his disciples turned back and no longer walked with him" (John 6:66).

They bail.

They wanted the free T-shirt, the Jesus jersey, the miracles, and the food. But they weren't willing to go wherever Jesus led. So they left. And instead of Jesus lightening his tone or begging them to come back and give him another chance, he simply lets them walk away.

Read what happens next.

> So Jesus said to the twelve, "Do you want to go away as well?" Simon

Peter answered him, "Lord, to whom shall we go? You have the words of eternal life, and we have believed, and have come to know, that you are the Holy One of God" (John 6:67-69).

I think if Jesus were standing with us tired dads today, he would call us to some hard things as well.

He'd invite us to die to ourselves. He'd tell us to lay down our lives to serve the ones he's put in our households. He'd demand that we put away our childish ways, grow up, and follow him wherever he leads us.

The truth is, many would hear those words and walk away. And just like he did back in the book of John, instead of softening his message, he'd turn to the rest of us and ask, "Do you want to go away as well?"

That's the question you'll have to answer for yourself. Do you want to leave? Did you come to Jesus for all the benefits he has to offer, or did you come to die?

> **Did you come to Jesus for all the benefits he has to offer, or did you come to die?**

Aspen is beautiful, but getting there isn't easy. The road to Nebraska is wider and probably easier to travel. Getting to the Aspen that God has called you to will require you to say no to a lot of things. It will mean giving up some things—even good things—so that you can say yes to the great things. It will mean sacrificing time with your friends. Giving up on some of your lifelong dreams. Choosing to get paid less. Laying down addictions that have tripped you up for years. Pursuing the heart of your kids even when they seem ungrateful and have no idea how much you've sacrificed.

The road to Aspen is hard. It's narrow. Few will take it. But for those who do, great is their reward—if not in this life, then in the one to come.

Here's the good news, man: Jesus never asked you to travel there alone. In fact, he said you can hitch a ride with him (Matthew 28:20). The road will be tough, but you're in good company. You have a good driver.

Jesus might be asking you, "Do you want to go away as well?" My prayer for you is that you'll look him right in the eye and say, "Not a chance. I'm all in."

I'll see you in Aspen, bro.

FINAL THOUGHTS

I've heard the chances of finishing a book are slim. A lot of people pick up a book and read a few chapters but never quite make it to the end. I want to personally say thank you for sticking with me. It means the world to me that you'd take the time to join me on this journey.

I'd hate for this to be the end of our time together. If you're interested in joining a group of guys who are trying to fall in love with Jesus so they can help their families do the same, we'd love to have you become part of the Dad Tired community.

I'm always hanging out on social media, and I'd love to meet you there or in person at one of our live events.

Finishing the book is one thing, but living it out is something else. Don't do it alone.

ABOUT THE AUTHOR

Jerrad Lopes is a Christian pastor and the founder of DadTired.com, a non-profit ministry focused on equipping men to lead their family well. He hosts the weekly *Dad Tired Podcast*, listened to by hundreds of thousands of men from around the world. He and his wife Leila live in Portland, Oregon with their three children.

ABOUT DAD TIRED

Dad Tired is a nonprofit ministry dedicated to helping
men lead their family well.

Join the thousands of men from around the world
who are taking their faith, family, and marriage very seriously.

www.dadtired.com

MORE GREAT HARVEST HOUSE BOOKS FOR DADS

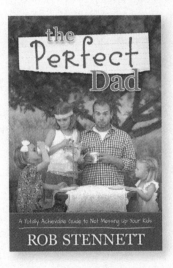

Great Dads Aren't Perfect...But They Aspire to Be

A father of four young girls, Rob Stennett is here to help you with some on-the-job training. With humor and thought-provoking honesty, Rob explores the 12 essential roles in your job description, including...

- *Provider*—Manage the stress of balancing work and family by establishing clear priorities at home and in your career.
- *Pastor*—Teach the wonder of Scripture and how your kids can cultivate a faith in God they love and cherish.
- *Husband*—Alleviate the pressure of modeling a healthy relationship for your kids by focusing on your spouse's needs first.
- *Counselor*—Help your kids avoid emotional pitfalls by becoming their most trusted source of wisdom.

You probably already know that becoming the perfect father is an unattainable goal, but that shouldn't stop you from trying your best to be a great dad. Your effort won't go unnoticed by your wife and kids. You can thrive in the most important job you've ever been given.

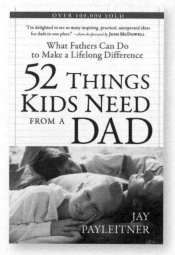

"God, please help me...another game of Candy Land..."

Jay Payleitner, veteran dad of five, has learned (with plenty of trial and error) how to build up his children's lives. *52 Things Kids Need from a Dad* combines straightforward features with step-up-to-the-mark challenges you'll appreciate:

- a full year's worth of focused, doable ideas
- uncomplicated ways to be an example, like "kiss your wife in the kitchen"
- tough, frank advice, like "throw away your porn"
- *no* exhausting lists of "things you should do"
- *no* criticism for acting like a man

You'll feel respected and empowered, and you'll gain confidence to initiate activities that build lifelong positives into your kids.

To learn more about Harvest House books and
to read sample chapters, visit our website:

www.harvesthousepublishers.com

HARVEST HOUSE PUBLISHERS
EUGENE, OREGON